# A
# CIVIL
# WAR
## POCKET
## READER

This edition published for Sweetwater Press
by arrangement with Cliff Road Books.

ISBN 1-58173-205-8

Copyright © 2002 by John Zwemer

Cover design: Connie Formby
Illustrations: *Authentic Civil War Illustrations*, Dover Publications, Inc.:
11, 29, 35, 61, 85, 113, 130, 133. Allison Moore: 57.

10     9     8     7     6     5     4     3     2     1

# A CIVIL WAR

# POCKET READER

Compiled by
**John Zwemer**

SWEET WATER PRESS

# Acknowledgments

To prepare acknowledgments leaves a writer concerned with inadvertently leaving a name from the "thank you" list. Should this occur, my humble apologies. To those names that follow, my deepest appreciation and regards.

Ellen Sullivan, Lee Howard, and Nina Costopoulos of Crane Hill Publishers, my thanks for believing in this project and for the many courtesies extended.

Allison Moore, Academic Magnet High School, Charleston, SC, class of 2002, my thanks for sketching the Quaker cannon.

Patrick Gorman, my sincerest appreciation for the thoughts expressed in the Foreword.

Esther Zwemer, my greatest appreciation for reading drafts, listening to stories, and being the "wings" of my life.

# CONTENTS

# FOREWORD

So you thought you knew all there was to know about the Civil War? Well, there is always something "new," something else, details forgotten —the ordinary and the not so ordinary that made up the texture of that time. Moments of drama and humor, everyday experiences, a reminder of the reality of the war of the rebellion—this is what *A Civil War Pocket Reader* will supply. Not descriptions of great strategies or battles, but incidents that force you to realize the simplicity, pain, humor, and humanity involved in the madness of civil war—a small window into that experience, if you will. Changing your frame of reference from the big picture to the personal, that is what interests me here, and I hope it will you as well.

*—Patrick Gorman*

# Introduction

"The world will never see their like again. As their ranks diminish, the reverence felt will increase." So declared a spectator at a gathering of Civil War veterans in 1903. Since the end of that tragic war, the Civil War soldier has held an emotional grip on successive generations of Americans. Their stories still speak to us today. Their bravery, devotion to duty, and love of country inspire us, entertain us, and humble us. This book gratefully acknowledges the memory of the Blue and Gray—Americans all.

The stories that follow are documented experiences from our nation's most tragic time. They are about real people, in real events. Spelling, grammar, and sentence structures are left as they appear in the original documents. The stories are related based upon the year in which they happened, from 1861 to 1865.

*—John Zwemer*

# 1 8 6 1

THE SOFT SOUTHERN MOONLIGHT
glistened down on the warm masonry.
Breezes filled the spring air with scent of
honeysuckle and magnolias. Waves caressed
the rock-strewn island. With a thunderous roar, a
cannon shot exploded over Fort Sumter, and life in
America was forever changed. Men who had been
shaking hands now shook their fists. Women who
had been sewing dresses turned to making flags
and caring for the wounded. Children dreamed of
faraway battlefields and fathers long from home.

When the nation awoke that April morning to
hear the news of Fort Sumter, the response was
the same no matter what side of the Mason-Dixon
Line the person was on—each individual was
ready to fight for home and country. War would
be so easy, just one mighty battle and the other
side would run for cover. Very few Americans
considered the cost in dollars and bodies this war
would render. However, all were ready to share in
this great adventure.

So high were the expectations in Washington
that a carnival-like atmosphere gripped the city.
Politicians, newspaper journalists, foreign military

observers, and, yes, even families packed food baskets and made the thirty-mile journey into the Virginia countryside to watch the Rebels "get their britches whipped." It was reported that some troops stopped to pick blackberries. It was a beautiful day for a picnic!

## TIME LINE

**9 January**    *Star of the West* supply vessel, heading for Charleston and Fort Sumter, is fired upon by cadets from The Citadel. The vessel is unable to land supplies.

**9 February**    Jefferson Davis is chosen provisional president of the Confederate States of America.

**4 March**    Abraham Lincoln is inaugurated as president of the United States.

**12 April**    Fort Sumter is fired upon by Confederate forces.

| | |
|---|---|
| **13 April** | The Federal garrison at Fort Sumter surrenders. |
| **14 April** | President Lincoln calls for 75,000 volunteers to put down the rebellion. |
| **20 April** | Robert E. Lee resigns from the United States Army. Lee will later accept a position in the Virginia (later Confederate) army. |
| **21 July** | Battle of Manassas (Bull Run) |
| **8 November** | British steamer *Trent* is stopped and boarded while upon high seas. Confederate emissaries are removed. This international incident threatens to bring Great Britain into the war. Lincoln determines "one war at a time." |

Speaking to Virginia Military Institute cadets on April 13, 1861, Thomas J. Jackson said, "...time for war has not yet come, but it will come and that soon, and when it does come, my advice is to draw the sword and throw away the scabbard." [1]

"So impatient did I become for starting, that I felt like ten thousand pins were pricking me in every part of my body."

—A Southern recruit, 1861 [2]

Impatience was not confined to Southerners. Thomas Southwick of New York was so overwhelmed with emotion after seeing a militia unit march down Broadway that when he caught sight of "the glorious old flag I shouted and yelled until I was hoarse. Tears gushed into my eyes and I turned away firmly resolved to defend that flag against any that would raise their hands against it, whether they were my countrymen or not." [3]

Strong Vincent of Erie, Pennsylvania (later to gain everlasting fame at Gettysburg) told his wife, "If I live, we will rejoice over our country's success.

If I fall, remember you have given your husband a sacrifice to the most glorious cause that ever widowed a woman." [4]

An officer of the 79th New York Highlanders went chasing after a pig while on the march to Bull Run. As he jumped over a rail fence, his kilt revealed his lack of underdrawers. The resultant laughter was so strong the officer never wore his kilt again. [5]

"They have killed me boys; but boys, NEVER! give it up."

—The words of dying Confederate Colonel Francis Bartow at First Manassas [6]

Proceeding toward the fighting at First Manassas, one of John Pelham's Confederates remarked as bullets clipped the trees: "Old Abe's splittin' rails again!" [7]

Burial parties came upon the body of a Federal soldier named Abbott. Abbott had been struck in the side by a spent cannon shot and the ball remained in his side. As the burial party removed the solid shot they discovered, to their amazement, that the foundry which cast the shot put advertising above the laws of ballistics and had imprinted the company name—ABBOTT—in the shot, and these letters were now imbedded in Abbott's flesh. [8]

After Stonewall Jackson told his men to give the Yankees "salt and pepper" at First Manassas, one of his men remarked, "that fellow is not much at cussing, but something in a fight!" [9]

Words of a soldier after Bull Run: "I shall see the thing played out or die in the attempt." [10]

Early in the war when news was slow in arriving, each letter home was eagerly awaited. Stonewall Jackson's minister received one letter from an illustrious church member. It read:

My dear Pastor,

In my tent last evening, after a fatiguing day's service, I remembered that I failed to

send you my contribution for our colored
Sunday School. Enclosed you will find a
check for that object, which please
acknowledge at your earliest convenience.
                    —(signed T. J. Jackson) [11]

Life for a soldier was filled with boredom
punctuated by moments of sheer terror. Many
soldiers found a fancy way of relieving the
boredom by staging louse or "grayback" races.
Most soldiers were infected with body lice. After
removing as many lice as possible from their
person, the men would place some of the creatures
on dinner plates and wager which louse might
"race" across the plate first. One enterprising
soldier named Dorin constantly won. His secret?
He always heated his plate before the race. [12]

During the Battle of Gaines Mill, Stonewall
Jackson had the opportunity to capture some
twenty Yankees. One of the prisoners recognized
"Ole Jack" and said to his fellows, "Gentlemen,
we have the honor of being captured by Stonewall
Jackson." [13]

The recruits during the war had to learn to obey without thinking, as one veteran wrote, "Some never do learn. I acquired it at last in humility and mud." [14]

Supplies and equipment were hard to come by for many units. Sterling Price's efforts to equip his Confederate army took on a rather novel approach. His men made their own ammunition. One-inch slugs cut from iron rods or old chains were fashioned into artillery canister; smooth stones replaced the solid shot! [15]

During the Confederate assault at Ball's Bluff, Colonel Nathan Evans, when not gaining inspiration from "above," invoked the aid of his canteen hanging at his side. [16]

Secret Service protection was not afforded Abraham Lincoln. Nevertheless, he was well guarded through most of the war. His old friend, Ward Lamon, took on the role of Lincoln's personal bodyguard. Lamon carried four pistols, two large knives, a blackjack, a pair of brass knuckles, and two very large fists! [17] (Lamon was not with Lincoln the night he was assassinated by John Wilkes Booth.)

Before leaving Richmond to take command at the Peninsula, Confederate General Joe Johnston was approached by Robert E. Lee, who worried about Johnston's habit of getting wounded. Lee held onto Joe for a length and then admonished him to take care of his life. [18]

Virginia Governor Letcher overheard a clerk in the Confederate war department comment that Stonewall Jackson was crazy. "Crazy! Crazy! It's a damned pity that Jackson's character or insanity does not attack some in this department!" retorted the Governor. [19]

"The patriotic volunteer, fighting for country and his rights, is the most reliable soldier on earth."

—Stonewall Jackson [20]

In the field it was quite difficult to obtain sugar or other sweet foods. Bob was always on the lookout for sweets. His messmates tired of his constant begging and stealing of their portions, so they devised a trick. A cup of sand that looked very similar to sugar was placed on the table. Bob came along and loaded up his cup of coffee with the sand. A fellow soldier indignantly rose up and remarked, "Bob, you great hog, I brought that sand to scour my gun, and you have nearly wasted it all." The whole company roared with laughter at the hapless sugar thief. [21]

During the early months of the war a young private from Tennessee was standing at evening picket duty. While peering through the night sky he thought he saw a Federal. Scared half stiff, the private did not know what to do. He challenged the Federal and got no response. Not wanting to wake the camp by firing his musket, the gallant boy from Tennessee charged the Federal and ran him through with the bayonet. To the Confederate's great relief and embarrassment, he had stuck a stump! [22]

Sam Watkins, of Company H in the 1st Tennessee Infantry recounts a shocking discovery. "At a little village called Hampshire Crossing [Virginia], our regiment was ordered to go to a little stream called St. John's Run, to relieve the 14th Georgia regiment and the 3rd Arkansas …when we arrived there we found the guard sure enough.…there were just eleven of them. Some were sitting down, and some were lying down; but each and every one was as cold and as hard frozen as the icicles that hung from their hands and faces and clothing—dead! They had died at their post of duty. Two of them, a little in advance of the others, were standing with their guns in their hands, as cold and as hard frozen as a monument of marble —standing sentinel with loaded guns in their frozen hands!" [23]

During the Battle of Belmont, Missouri, a Federal officer noticed a gallant Confederate, conspicuous in his bravery. The Federal shot at the man, who went down. The next day the Federal officer returned to the spot and, looking at the body, discovered that he had shot and killed his own brother. [24]

While inspecting camp one evening, a general came upon a sentinel. The general began to question the man:

"What would you do if you saw two men coming towards you?"

"I would halt them and direct one to give the countersign."

"What would you do if several men came at you?"

"The same thing sir."

"Well, what if a whole regiment were coming down the road?"

"Well, sir, I would make a line."

"A line?"

"Yes, Sir! A Bee line for camp!" [25]

A Federal officer, noted for his lively wit, approached a party of lovely Southern belles. "If all the young ladies down here are as lovely as you, I'll have no part in conquering the Confederacy." To which one of the belles replied, "Well, sir, if all the gentlemen in your army are as ugly as you are, we ladies have no desire to conquer them!" [26]

Many a young soldier, having never seen salt water, would appreciate the prank pulled on a Mississippi recruit. It seems this fellow went down to the Gulf of Mexico shoreline and pulled himself a bucket of water with which to wash his face. Leaving the bucket for a few minutes, he returned and was mightily shocked when the salt water hit his eyes. He stormed off shouting, "A man can't draw a bucket of water, and leave it for a few minutes, without some prank is played upon him!" His comrades doubled over with laughter. 27

A soldier, while on leave in Richmond, was walking down a street when he chanced upon President Jefferson Davis. "Sir, Mister, Being you Jefferson Davis?" The president replied that he was the man. To which the soldier replied, "I thought so, sir, beings you look so much like a Confederate postage stamp." 28

Jimmy Ferris was determined to get himself a pair of boots. Following the battle he went out and began to search among the dead Yankees. He came upon a body that appeared to be of his size. Pulling on the boots, Jimmy set to his task of obtaining footwear. At that moment the body groaned, and Jimmy dropped the boots in a hurry and ran for cover. After some anxious minutes, Jimmy got up nerve to try again. Finding another corpse, he approached it gingerly and inquired, "Mr. Yankee, are you dead?" [29]

From Elisha Hunt Rhodes, Company D, 2nd Rhode Island Infantry: "December 30, 1861. This afternoon, seeing the general alone in the office, I stepped up to him and said:

'General, I want to go home.'

'Want to go home, and for what?' he replied.

'I want to see my mother.'

'Is she ill?'

'No, I hope not.'

He then asked me how long since I had left home and if I was ever away for so long a time before. I told him I had been in the service seven months and never been away from home alone before.

'Well, You have been a good boy, and you shall have a furlough for ten days.' " 30

Soldiers were very ingenious when trying to escape the notice of the provost Guard. One company of Mississippi troops wanted very much to have some spirituous refreshment in its camp. Knowing the provost would be looking out for such refreshment, the men stopped by a watermelon patch and procured a large melon. They cut a plug in the melon, poured the liquid refreshment inside, replaced the plug and strode confidently into camp. The soldiers then dug a small pit in the floor of one tent, placed the melon there, and inserted straws. What a refreshing pause those soldiers enjoyed. 31

"Skirmishing with graybacks" was a well-regarded activity with troops. It mattered not whether a soldier was a "graduate from Harvard [or] illiterate from the wilds of Maine"...multitudes of soldiers were often seen pinching the lice between thumb and forefinger, many times assisting each other with the chore. 32

President Lincoln would sometimes travel about visiting the troops unattended. On one occasion, Mr. Lincoln attempted to walk into a headquarters tent when he was stopped by a guard who said: "We do not allow citizens to pass, especially sanitary fellows." (The sanitary commission was an early version of the Red Cross.) [33]

A young "greenhorn" Confederate was placed on guard duty. As the night deepened, an owl began to "Who-Who." The young soldier answered back, "It's me, sir, John Albert, a friend of yours!" [34]

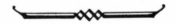

THE FIRST BATTLES ENDED ALL HOPES FOR quick, easy victories. Both sides settled in for a long, drawn-out war. The glamour and romance of fighting gave way to the harsh reality of muddy, disease-filled camps, long days of endless drilling, and lonely nights on picket duty. Yet brave Americans, regardless of political persuasion, were in this conflict to the end. Their cause was worth fighting for, even dying for. No stain would be placed upon their stones.

# 1862

THE SIGHT OF SPECTATORS AT FIRST Manassas seems foreign to modern readers, but what a thrill those nineteenth-century folks must have envisioned. It was not to be. Following such a bloody introduction to war, there were no more spectators, just men doing the awful business of killing.

Adventures aside, both armies got down to training troops for the rugged nature of fighting en masse. Days turned into weeks and then into months. Many a homesick lad would wonder if he would ever escape the wrath of the drill sergeant. Back and forth across muddy or dusty fields they would trudge, musket drill in the morning, bayonet practice in the afternoon. Cleaning weapons by campfire, and maybe a moment to pen a letter to loved ones far away, would close the day for the weary soldiers.

The second year of the war brought forth the "march on Richmond." George McClelland's huge army was set in motion, hoping to make those troublesome Rebs wish they had left well enough alone. Out west, a hard-luck former West Pointer was beginning to show the grit and determination so lacking in other Union leaders, while in the east, a Virginia gentleman had yet to gain the glory which would later canonize him for eternity.

## TIME LINE

**15 February**    Ulysses S. Grant obtains the unconditional surrender of Fort Henry and Fort Donaldson in Tennessee.

**9 March**    Naval engagement between USS *Monitor* and the CSS *Virginia* (*Merrimac*) is the first combat between iron vessels.

**6 April**    Battle of Shiloh (Pittsburg Landing) in Tennessee

**12 April**    Great Locomotive Chase. Union spies steal a train and attempt to destroy the railroad between Atlanta and Chattanooga. Although they failed, the men were the first to receive the newly created Medal of Honor.

**25 April**    New Orleans falls to Federal forces.

| | |
|---|---|
| **25 June** | Battle of Seven Pines; beginning of the Seven Days battles in Virginia |
| **27 June** | Battle of Gaines Mill, Virginia |
| **28 June** | Battle of Garnett's Farm, Virginia |
| **29 June** | Battle of Savage Station, Virginia |
| **1 July** | Battle of Malvern Hill, Virginia |
| **8 August** | Battle of Cedar Mountain, Virginia |
| **29 August** | Battle of Second Manassas (Bull Run) |
| **17 September** | Battle of Sharpsburg (Antietam), considered the bloodiest single day of the entire war |
| **8 October** | Battle of Perryville, Kentucky |
| **22 October** | Battle of Pea Ridge, Arkansas |
| **13 December** | Battle of Fredericksburg, Virginia |
| **31 December** | Battle of Murfreesboro (Stone's River), Tennessee |

"I had a Sergeant Driscoll, a brave man, one of the best shots in the Brigade. When charging Malvern Hill (July 1, 1862), a company was posted in a clump of trees, which kept up a fierce fire on us, and actually charged out on our advance. Their officer seemed to be a daring, reckless boy, and I said to Driscoll, 'If that officer is not taken down, many of us will fall before we pass that clump.'

'Leave that to me,' said Driscoll; so he raised his rifle, and the moment the officer was visible again, bang went Driscoll; and down went the officer, his company breaking away.

As we passed the place, I said, 'Driscoll, see if that officer is dead—he was a brave fellow.' I stood looking on. Driscoll turned him over on his back. The officer opened his eyes for a moment and faintly murmured, 'Father' and closed them forever.

I will forever recollect the frantic grief of Driscoll; it was harrowing to witness. The officer was his son, who had gone South before the war.

We were soon ordered to charge, and I left Driscoll there but, as we were closing in on the enemy, he rushed up with coat off, and clutching his musket, charged right up on the enemy, calling the men to follow. He soon fell but jumped up again. We knew he was wounded. On he dashed but soon rolled over like a top. When we came up he was dead, riddled with bullets."

—Captain D.P. Conyngham, Federal staff officer [35]

Military regulations forbade the use of liquor, however many soldiers including generals used spirituous liquids to ease the boredom and loneliness of camp life. One such experience occurred during the Peninsular campaign of 1862. Confederate General John B. Magruder, while ordering his men to observe the ban on liquor, was not opposed to having a "smile" now and again. One fine Virginia morning, General Magruder noticed a soldier walking in such manner as to arouse suspicion. "Halt. What is your name and what is in your canteen?" cried the general.

"Water, sir, and my name is Private Sharpe," answered the soldier.

"Well, sir, give me your water, sir," replied the general.

With trembling hands, Sharpe offered up his canteen, knowing that the contents were most definitely not water. General Magruder took a long pull on the canteen and returned it.

"You, sir, are no longer Private Sharpe, but Corporal Sharpe, and thank you for the 'water.' "

Now Sharpe, being a sharp fellow, decided to hang around the general's tent. Later that morning the general called, "Corporal Sharpe, may I have your canteen, sir?"

"Certainly, sir." Again the general took a long pull.

"You, sir, are no longer Corporal Sharpe, but are now Sergeant Sharpe, and thank you for your water." Sharpe was beginning to see grand and glorious things ahead in his life so he resolved to stay by the general the remainder of the day. In middle afternoon the general had another hankering for water and called to Sergeant Sharpe, "Sir, another drink of your water."

"Of course, general." Again the general "smiled" and as he returned the canteen said, "You are no longer Sergeant Sharpe, but Lieutenant Sharpe, and thank you for your water." Sharpe was now convinced that he was on the road to greatness, but to his horror and great dismay, found his canteen empty. The rest of the day was spent in frantic search of the camp for some more water. None could be found. Toward evening, General Magruder called again for Sharpe.

Lieutenant Sharpe answered the general, "Sir, it is with deep regret that I inform you that the water is all played out, but Sir, if I had some more I'll be damned if I wouldn't go to bed a brigadier general!" [36]

Confederate General John B. Magruder loved amateur plays, and while in command along the Peninsula he produced a remarkable performance. With only a few hundred men, he marched them through a thicket and into an opening time and again, fooling the Yankees into thinking they were facing a whole host of rebels. [37]

While riding in Thaddeus Lowe's hot-air balloon over the Peninsula, Federal General Fitz-John Porter had the misfortune of the balloon breaking its tether and drifting over toward enemy lines. Porter climbed up, released the gas valve, and landed safely on a Federal tent. [38]

To give his wavering troops confidence, Confederate General D. H. Hill rode slowly through enemy fire calmly smoking his cigar. [39]

Many officers on both sides of this war knew each other from the prewar army. Ulysses Grant liked to recall a story about his opponent Braxton Bragg. Bragg was notorious for his bad temper and inflexibility. Bragg was once on duty both as company commander and quartermaster. As company commander, he demanded certain supplies; as quartermaster, he refused. He continued an angry exchange of memorandums in his two roles and finally referred the matter to his post commander. That officer cried, "My God! Bragg! You have quarreled with every officer in the Army and now you are quarreling with yourself!" [40]

Mud was such a problem on the Peninsula the following story made the rounds in the Federal army. "A mule and its wagon were swallowed up to the mule's ears by the horrific mud." Well, it was a small mule. [41]

William Pendleton, Chief of the Army of Northern Virginia artillery, was also an ordained minister. Pendleton conducted services in the field when not in combat. He was overheard once as Federal troops advanced on his guns: "While we kill their bodies, may the Lord have mercy on their souls—Fire!" [42]

Watching his men wavering at the White Oak Swamp, Confederate General A. P. Hill shouted, "Damn you, if you will not follow me, I'll die alone!" Thrilled by the general's outrage, his men charged, repulsing the Federal attack. [43]

During the war some soldiers tried to escape duty by pretending to be sick or crazy. One such soldier played this game quite successfully. Early one morning following a heavy rain, the soldier tied a string to his bayonet, took a position on the parapet, began fishing in a shallow pool, and to all appearances became quite unmindful of his surroundings.

Some minutes passed. No one bothered him, and he could be seen regularly lifting his musket and checking his line. This procedure went on as the rest of the camp went about normal morning routine. It was soon apparent to all that something was lacking in the "head-work" of this soldier.

The other fellows in the camp began to gather around and poke fun at the busy fisherman, but he paid them no mind and went about the business of checking the line and recasting into the muddy pond. By and by the captain came up, "What are you doing here?" demanded the officer. No response. The fisherman again examined the fishing pole and string.

"Halt!" cried the captain, hoping a familiar command would bring the fisherman to his senses.

No response.

"Shoulder arms!"

Again the fisherman was too intent on his pole to notice the familiar order. The captain decided to call the surgeon, who came and examined the fisherman, as best he could, for the fisherman went about the continued business of raising and lowering the musket, bayonet, and string.

The surgeon determined the man to be insane and wrote out a medical discharge on the spot. The surgeon handed the discharge to the captain, but before giving it to the soldier, the surgeon asked, "What are you fishing for?"

No answer.

"Well, I guess you can give him the papers," stated the surgeon, and the captain handed them over to the fisherman, saying loudly, "Here! Take these papers!"

"That's what I was fishing for!" replied the fisherman as he threw down his pole, pocketed the papers, and raced out the entrance to the camp, much to the amazement of the surgeon and captain, and to the great amusement of his fellow soldiers. [44]

Following the unqualified success of the ironclad USS *Monitor*, the London magazine *Punch* declared: "the old seaman's expression 'shiver my timbers' would be changed to 'unrivet my bolts!' " [45]

During a sharp engagement Federal General Phil Kearny rode through his hesitating troops and shouted, "Don't flinch boys, they're shooting at me, not you!" With a laugh and shout his men went forward. [46]

Astride his horse at Seven Pines, Joe Johnston was an impressive figure. He calmed his men by saying, "…There is no use of dodging; when you hear them they have passed." Moments later, a shell fragment unhorsed Johnston. [47]

Federal General William French fell into a deep mud hole while directing his men at Seven Pines. A captain hollered, "The general will be drowned!" The thought of a general drowning while the bullets whistled overhead brought forth a huge roar of laughter from the troops. French was retrieved, wet, mud-covered, and mad. [48]

Federal General Oliver Howard lost his right arm at the Battle of Seven Pines. While recovering he was visited by General Phil Kearny, who was lacking his left arm. "There is one thing we can do together general," Kearny consoled his friend, "we can buy our gloves together!" [49]

Robert E. Lee was widely considered to be the spiritual heir to George Washington, and some friends thought he consciously acted out the role. Governor Letcher once teased Lee by saying, "General Lee, you certainly play Washington to perfection." [50]

D. H. Hill sat calmly underneath a tree near the fighting at Glendale. An officer begged Hill to take better cover. Hill retorted, "Don't worry about me; look after the men. I am not going to be killed until my time comes." Just then a shell exploded close to the officer, lifting him up and covering him with dirt. Shaking the dirt from his clothes, Hill took his seat on the other side of the tree. [51]

President Lincoln went out to review the troops. A chaplain in a Connecticut regiment wrote:

"We were called into line and he went the rounds. I have seldom witnessed a more ludicrous sight than our worthy Chief Magistrate presented on horseback. While I lifted my cap with respect for the man raised up by God to rule our troubled times, I lowered it speedily to cover a smile that overmastered me. It did seem as though every moment the President's legs would become entangled with those of the horse and both come down together." [52]

Another view of Lincoln comes from Lieutenant James Abrahams:

"As he (Lincoln) passed along the lines his black cloth and high plug hat contrasted strangely with the gold and glitter of McClellan and his staff, but he seemed to look right into the soul of each individual soldier and although he uttered not a word, yet he left an abiding impression that he was our fast and sympathizing friend." [53]

Blue, gray, and butternut are colors we associate with North and South. At Shiloh one regiment of Confederates went into battle wearing wool that had not yet been dyed. It was later asked, "Who were those hell-cats that went into battle dressed in their graveclothes?" [54]

As Confederate troops moved into Lexington, Kentucky, Ella Bishop endeared herself to the Unionists of the town. Ella marched into the street and rescued a large U.S. flag the Confederates were dragging through town. Ella wrapped the flag around her body and declared the flag would only leave her person with her life. She was left unharmed. [55]

James and William Terrill, sons of Virginia, made the heartrending decision so prevalant during the war. James became a brigadier in the Confederate army and William stood by the Union. Both lost their lives during the war. Afterwards the family erected a monument on which they had these words carved: "God Alone Knows Which Was Right." [56]

Leonidas Polk served not only as an Episcopal bishop but also as a Confederate general. During the campaigning in Tennessee, Polk was riding near the front lines as darkness made visibility difficult. Thinking the troops firing into the twilight were from his command, Polk ordered them to cease firing. The colonel in charge replied he was certain he was firing on the enemy. Polk still wished for firing to halt and asked the colonel for his name. The colonel replied with the additive that his was an Indiana regiment and inquired who Polk was!

Polk boldly replied: "I'll soon show you who I am, cease fire at once!" Thinking he would be shot down in a volley, Polk turned back to his proper lines unscathed. [57]

After the second Battle of Manassas (Bull Run), the hospitals of Washington were filled with wounded Federals and Confederates. President Lincoln journeyed to a hospital to visit with and pray for the suffering men. After spending nearly the entire day with the wounded, the President knelt and prayed by the cot of a very young, dying Confederate.

Tired and worn, the President stepped to his carriage. A nurse came running to President Lincoln to say that the dying boy was pleading to see him again. As tired as Lincoln was, he returned to the boy's side and asked, "What might I do for you?"

"I am so lonely and friendless," whispered the boy, "and I am hoping that you can tell me what my mother would want me to say and do now."

"Yes, my boy," said the President, as he knelt by the boy's cot. "I know exactly what your mother would want you to say and do. And I am glad that you sent for me to come back to you. Now as I kneel here, please repeat the words after me."

Then, as the dying boy rested his head upon the arm of President Lincoln, he repeated the words his mother had taught him:

*Now I lay me down to sleep,*
*I pray the Lord my soul to keep.*
*If I should die before I wake,*
*I pray the Lord my soul to take.*
*And this I ask for Jesus' sake.* [58]

As triumphant Southerners raced past his cannon during Second Manassas, Northern Captain Mark Kerns called out, "I promised to drive you back or die under my guns, and I have kept my word." Kerns died shortly thereafter. [59]

A private soldier went up to George Townsend, a reporter for the *New York Herald*, and asked if Townsend would write a short dictated letter. It read:

"My dear Mary, we are going into action soon, and I send you my love. Kiss baby, and if I am not killed I will write to you after the fight."

The same post that carried his letter also carried the news of his death. [60]

Scurvy became a real threat to soldiers in the field. Northern care societies encouraged families to send not only letters but also food. One popular poster urged: "Don't send your sweetheart a love-letter, send him an onion." [61]

The shrill voice of a boy sobbing was heard at the battle at Brawner's Farm, (part of the fighting at Second Manassas). The boy's father was the captain of the company. As the father reached the wounded lad, the boy called out, "Father, my leg is broken but I don't want you to think that is what I am crying for; I fell in a yellow-jacket's nest and they have been stinging me ever since. That is what makes me cry—please pull me out." The stings and wound proved too much for the plucky boy and he died shortly thereafter in his father's arms. [62]

The words of Captain David Gibson of the 3rd West Virginia Infantry: "Major, I shall be killed in this charge. I tell you I am going to be killed in this charge, I knew it last night, I have known it all morning." Gibson was killed in a charge later that same day. [63]

It is easy to forget that women, too, faced the terrors of the battlefield. Clara Barton recalled the horror of Antietam:

"A man lying on the ground asked for a drink, I stooped to give it, and having raised him with my right hand, was holding the cup to his lips with my left, when I felt a sudden twitch of the loose sleeve of my dress. The poor fellow sprang from my hands and fell back quivering, in the agonies of death. A ball had passed between my body and the right arm which supported him cutting through the sleeve, and passing through his chest from shoulder to shoulder." [64]

As the Confederates swept Chinn Ridge clear of Yankees, an old farmer rode up excitedly waving his arms. "Go on my boys, and you'll end this war. The Yankees are running like hell." [65]

"Lord bless your dirty ragged souls!" The words of an old female resident of Leesburg, Virginia, spoken as the Army of Northern Virginia moved towards its date with destiny at Sharpsburg. [66]

As Stonewall Jackson's reputation grew, many stories about him were passed around the campfire. A favorite of the troops was regarding the telegram received from the devil himself begging Jackson to stop killing Yankees as he (the devil) had run out of room to place them! [67]

A resident of Middleton, Maryland, inquired why the Confederate troops were so ragged looking. The reply came: "Our mammas always taught us to put on our worst clothes when we go to kill hogs!" [68]

When asked why the Confederates lacked shoes, a jaunty Confederate acknowledged, "We wore out our shoes running after the Yankees." To which an old man took off his shoes and gave them to a barefooted Southerner. [69]

A chaplain of one of the regiments was conspicuous for his pair of bearskin leggings. During the fighting at Fox's Gap, near Sharpsburg, the parson was seen bounding over the tops of the laurel bushes like a kangaroo. A member of the regiment saw the parson running for the rear and exclaimed in facetious voice that could be heard above the noise of battle, "Parson, parson—Damn it, come back here; you have been praying all your life to get to heaven and now that you have a chance for a short cut you are running away from it." [70]

During the fighting at Crampton's Pass, a Federal soldier fell into a crevice to find a Confederate already there. Both men glared at each other until the Rebel burst out, "We're both in a fix, I can't gobble you, nor you me. Let's wait till the shooting is over, and if your side wins I'm your prisoner, and if we win you're my prisoner." [71]

As the fighting raged around Antietam Creek, two German brothers marched towards the Rebels. First one brother fell victim of a sharpshooter. "There is the man who killed my brother," the other brother remarked calmly, "and he is taking aim now against that tree." Moments later the second brother fell dead. [72]

When George McClellan was replaced a second time by President Lincoln, Robert E. Lee was heard to remark, "I fear they may continue to make these changes till they find someone whom I don't understand." [73]

It was so cold the winter of 1862 that Stonewall Jackson's quartermaster recalled the ink froze in his jacket inkstand as he was preparing the daily reports. [74]

The evening of December 10, 1862, the Union and Confederate armies glared at each other across the Rappahannock River. Then the Federal band began to play. First it played "Hail Columbia" then "Star Spangled Banner," "Yankee Doodle," and other patriotic airs. Hearing no responses from the Southern side, the Federals then played "Dixie." It was then that cheers and shouts of merriment floated over the river as men from both sides enjoyed the concert. [75]

Stonewall Jackson's men were under strict orders not to reveal information or plans to anyone. When asked, "What division do you belong to?" one soldier replied, "Don't know!" The question came back, "What brigade?" "Don't know that either." "Well, what regiment?" The soldier replied: "All I know ole Stonewall ordered me not to know anything, and damned if I ain't going to stick to it!" [76]

Snowball fighting was quite a treat for soldiers from the Deep South. A brigade of Texas soldiers got into the spirit so much that when General James Longstreet rode nearby he was pelted with snow. Longstreet did not take too kindly to this affront of his dignity and hollered at the men:

"Throw your snowballs men, if you want to, as much as you please; but, if one of them touches me, not a man in this brigade shall have a furlough this winter. Remember that." [77]

A Confederate courier, during the battle at Shiloh, lost his horse, got on a mule he captured, and charged ahead of his company. He began to seesaw on the mule and grit his teeth, and finally shouted out, "It ain't me boys, it's this blasted mule. Whoa, mule!" [78]

Following the sixth charge at the stone wall of Fredericksburg, a soldier was seen to be standing with a cartridge in his teeth, just gazing out at the Federals. "My good man, I don't think they're coming again," cried out his sergeant. There was no response, for the soldier had a bullet through his head. He died and "froze" in the act of tearing his cartridge. [79]

A Federal soldier tells of a gentlemen's agreement: "General Thomas J. Jackson came down to the river bank today with a party of ladies and officers. We raised our hats to the party and strange to say the ladies waved their handkerchiefs in reply....We could have shot him with a revolver, but we had an agreement that neither side will fire, as it does no good, and in fact is simply murder." [80]

While advancing on the Confederate lines at Fredericksburg, the Irish members of the 24th Georgia regiment recognized the green flag of the Irish Brigade. "What a pity. Here come Meagher's (Irish Brigade commander) fellows." The Irish Georgians took aim and mowed down their fellow Irishmen. [81]

"Always mystify, mislead, and surprise the enemy if possible."

—Thomas J. Jackson [82]

Some North Carolina pickets had been watching a dwelling across the river from their lines. The house appeared to be the headquarters for some high-ranking Federal officer. The Carolinians decided to make a so-called Quaker cannon. They assembled wagon wheels, a hollow log, a rammer, and a large stone.

The Confederates raced the "gun" to the river, wheeled it into position and pointed it at the headquarters. With loud commands they rammed the stone into the log and seemed ready to destroy the dwelling. The Federal pickets raced around preparing for action and speedily emptied the house. Presently the joke was determined by all and, with much merriment, both sides went back to business. [83]

*Quaker cannon*

Confederate General Lloyd Tilghman, commander of Fort Henry, fought bravely before surrendering his post. When he came on board the flagship of Federal Flag Officer Andrew Foote, Foote said, "Come, General, you have lost your dinner, and the steward has just told me that mine is ready." The two men walked together into the cabin. [84]

General Grant's table may have suited Lloyd Tilghman, but it did not impress Grant's young son Fred. Fred often ate with the enlisted men that were much better at foraging than General Grant. [85]

As the terrible Battle of Shiloh raged, a rabbit trembling with fear rushed out of the bushes and snuggled up close to a soldier. [86]

The crossing of the Confederate Army into Maryland in 1862 was stopped when a balky team of mules created a traffic jam. On the Virginia shore, Stonewall Jackson called for Quartermaster John Harman, who rode out into the tangle of wagons and let loose a resounding blast of curses. Hearing the volcanic fury of the major, the mules dashed for Maryland. Harman rode back to Jackson, expecting a sermon from the pious commander. "General, the ford is clear, there is only one language that mules will understand on a hot day, they must get out of the water!" To everyone's surprise, Jackson grinned. [87]

Federal Colonel Francis Barlow was so tired of his drummers shirking their duty that before going into battle at Antietam he tied them to his sash and led them forward under fire. [88]

Just before the 3rd Arkansas stepped into the fray at Sharpsburg, a member of the regiment requested permission to "kinda give the boys a tune as they move out? I got my fiddle with me." The captain agreed, and asked for the mountain tune, "Granny, Will Your Dog Bite? Hellfire, No!" With the fiddler in the lead the 3rd Arkansas went forth to meet the enemy. [89]

As General Thomas Woods moved forward into the fight at Stone's River, Tennessee, he remarked to General Thomas Crittenden, "Goodbye, general; we'll meet at the hatter's, as one coon said to another when the dogs were after them." [90]

Sam Watkins recalled the vicious fighting at Stone's River, which resulted in the wounding of a comrade. "His face was as white as a sheet. The frazzled end of his shirtsleeve appeared to be sucked into the wound. I said 'Great God' for I could see his heart throb and the respiration of his lungs. He was walking along, when all of a sudden he dropped down and died without a struggle or groan." [91]

THE FIRST FULL YEAR OF CONFLICT CLOSED with the combatants flushed with gleams of victory. Yet the tugs of sadness that would eventually engulf the country began to focus pain in communities throughout the nation. Men were making the fateful choice to either "see this through to the end" or pass the torch of freedom to another's hand.

# 1863

THE THIRD YEAR OF THE WAR OPENED with the stunning Confederate victory at Chancellorsville and the staggering news of Stonewall Jackson's death. The summer brought tidings of Gettysburg and Vicksburg. Confederate hopes that began so high were beginning to fade, and the rising stars of Grant, Sherman, and Sheridan were sparkling in the Federal eyes.

## TIME LINE

**1 January**   Emancipation Proclamation goes into effect.

**2 January**   Battle of Murfreesboro continues along the banks of the Stone's River in Tennessee.

**1 May**   Battle of Chancellorsville begins in Virginia.

**2 May**   Stonewall Jackson is accidentally shot.

**10 May**   Stonewall Jackson dies.

| | |
|---|---|
| **28 May** | 54th Massachusetts Colored Infantry leaves for action. This is the first fully trained black regiment in the Union army. |
| **1 July** | Battle of Gettysburg, Pennsylvania, begins. |
| **3 July** | Climactic end to fighting at Gettysburg with the charge of Pickett, Pettigrew, and Trimble's divisions against the Federal center. Recalled by many observers as the "high-water mark of Confederacy." |
| **4 July** | Vicksburg, Mississippi, surrenders. |
| **18 July** | 54th Massachusetts Colored Infantry attempts an assault of Battery Wagner outside Charleston, South Carolina. |
| **19 September** | Battle of Chickamauga, Georgia |
| **19 November** | President Lincoln delivers the Gettysburg Address. |
| **23 November** | Battle of Chattanooga, Tennessee |

Stonewall Jackson rarely drew his sword. When he was rallying his men at Cedar Mountain, Jackson found his sword rusted into the scabbard. Unhooking it from his belt, Jackson waved the sword and scabbard over his head as he led his troops back to the fight. [92]

General Jackson's popularity with the troops grew to such heights that the remark was made that whenever shouting was heard in camp it was either "...Jackson or a rabbit." [93]

During the fighting at Chancellorsville, General A. W. Whipple was shot near the heart and died. His men professed great surprise that a ball could penetrate the layers of dirt covering the general's body. He was so filthy as to be considered invulnerable. [94]

After the Southern army crossed over into Maryland, a Union loyalist remarked:

"...Were these dirty, lank, ugly specimens of humanity the men that had driven back again and again our splendid legions with their fine discipline, their martial show and color? I felt humiliated at the thought that this horde of ragamuffins could set our grand army of the Union at defiance. Oh, they are so dirty! I don't think the Potomac River could wash them clean!" [95]

John Mosby's guerrilla tactics were legendary, but none of them quite topped the capture of General Edwin Stoughton. General Stoughton, having enjoyed a night of champagne and young ladies, was sleeping soundly in his Fairfax, Virginia, headquarters when Mosby managed to slip past the guards. Mosby found the general blissfully snoring. Slapping the general's buttocks, Mosby declared: "Get up, General, and come with me."

Sleepily, Stoughton looked into the strange face and asked for the meaning of the intrusion.

"Did you ever hear of Mosby?"

"Yes, have you caught him?"

"No, but he has caught you!"

With that, Edwin Stoughton and thirty of his troops were captured. After a few months in confinement Stoughton was exchanged, whereupon he resigned from the Federal army. [96]

Another Union resident echoed the thoughts about the dirty Confederates, but noted, "... there was a dash about them that the northern men lacked." [97]

"Does it not make the General proud to see how these men love him?"

"Not proud, it 'awes' him."

—Conversation between two of Robert E. Lee's staff [98]

As the brave Rebels marched farther into Maryland, a young, buxom lady stood by the road watching the ragged troops passing by. Noticing a Union pin on her blouse, a boy from Louisiana called out, "Look h'yar, miss, better take that flag down, we're awful fond of charging breast works." The lady blushed, but the pin remained defiantly pinned to her clothing. [99]

Chaplain William Locke, 11th Pennsylvania Infantry, noticed a young girl standing by her Culpepper, Virginia, home. As the girl viewed the retreating Yankees she gaily called out, "Goodbye, Yankees. I'm glad you're going." [100]

General Stonewall Jackson was noted for many eccentricities, none more than a twitch he developed as battle approached. Observers could not determine whether it was nerves or resolve. The soldiers thought "Old Jack is making faces at the Yankees." [101]

One of Jackson's men exclaimed, "I wish the Yankees were in Hell!" To which came a comrade's retort: "I don't. Old Jack would follow them there, with our brigade in front!" The first one continued, "Well, that's so, Bill, but I wish the Yankees were in Heaven. They're too good for this earth!" "I don't, because Jack would follow them there, too, and as it's our turn to go on picket, we wouldn't enjoy ourselves a bit!" [102]

Thomas J. Jackson was, if anything, a precise and dedicated Christian. Throughout his service to the Confederate army there is no record of any correspondence bearing a Sunday postmark. He not only preached but also lived his faith. [103]

While his men were fording the chilly Rapidan River, Confederate General Joe Kershaw proclaimed, "Go ahead, boys, don't mind this." The general was mounted on his horse and continued to remind the troops about his days in Mexico. "General," the men shouted back, "it wasn't so cold in Mexico!" [104]

"Did you ever think, sir, what an opportunity a battlefield affords liars?"
—Stonewall Jackson to a staff officer [105]

Note attached to a miniature boat used to transfer items between the pickets along the Rappahannock River: "I send you some tobacco and expect some coffee in return send me some postage stamps you will oblige, your rebel." [106]

"Mamma I dream about you all nearly every night…and think about you every hour in the day."
—From a letter written by Eli Landers, 16th Georgia Infantry [107]

A "greenhorn Yankee" professed that when the bullets began to fly, he would run to the rear. As his captain was later checking on the men during the height of the fighting, the professed "coward" was slowly loading his musket and said very calmly, "I believe the powder goes in first, don't it?" [108]

Following the engagement at Chancellorsville, General Joseph Hooker wrote President Lincoln, "…no general battle was fought at Chancellorsville and we lost no honor at Chancellorsville." Is it any wonder Mr. Lincoln was heard to say "My god! What will the country say?" [109]

E. Porter Alexander's family lived within the sounds of the fighting at Chancellorsville. His eighteen-month-old daughter remarked, "Hear my papa shoot Yankee. BOO!" [110]

"I have been tried and condemned without a hearing, and I suppose I shall have to go to the execution."
> —George Meade upon hearing of his elevation to command of the Army of the Potomac in late June 1863 [111]

During the first day's battle for Gettysburg, Federal Lieutenant Bayard Wilkerson's right leg was nearly severed. Wilkerson calmly used his pocketknife to cut the mangled leg off, using his sash as a tourniquet. He died hours later. [112]

Confederate General Richard Ewell had lost a leg earlier in the war. While observing the action on July 1, Ewell was struck again, and he commented: "It don't hurt a bit to be shot in a wooden leg." [113]

On the third day of Gettysburg, while awaiting the signal to begin Pickett's Charge, a rabbit was seen leaving the battle area in a great hurry. A grizzled soldier hollered after the rabbit, "Run, rabbit, run! If I was an ole' rabbit I'd run, too!" [114]

During the Confederate withdrawal from Pickett's Charge, General Robert E. Lee came upon a wounded Federal. The Federal yelled out, "Hurrah for the Union!"

General Lee heard the shout, stopped his horse, dismounted, and went to the soldier. General Lee looked down on the soldier with great tenderness and, grasping the man's hand, said, "My son, I hope you will soon be well."

Years later, the soldier related that he cried himself to sleep that night, not from the pain of his wound, but from the shame he felt for having tried to ridicule such a great man. [115]

General Lee was noted for his kindness. Before serving up portions of corn pone and bacon, Lee cut off a thick slice for his attendant who, according to the general, had "…harder work than we have…." [116]

"In some way Major Robbins had secured about a handful of peas. We boiled his peas and my bacon in an oyster can, and there with the Major's two potatoes, which he kindly divided with me, was the menu of the Field and Staff of the 4th Alabama that night."

> —Robert Coles, 4th Alabama, outside Chattanooga in 1863 [117]

Irving Buck, of Patrick Cleburne's staff, agreed with a fellow officer's lecture on the need to be more spiritual. Buck's first prayer began:

"Headquarters, Cleburne's Division, Hardee's Corps." Reading this typical heading for all orders and correspondence was a force of habit as Buck later recalled. [118]

Sophia McClelland administrated the U.S. Sanitary Commission during the fighting in western Tennessee. She recalled a Confederate who was very grateful for a sip of water. The man gasped, "Good! I should say it was. I've been crying for it for six hours, and I never thought I'd be crying for water. Anyhow, not to drink! But this blamed war has upset things so that there ain't no telling what a man will do!" [119]

"Home, boys. Home! Remember, home is over beyond those hills!"

> —Words of an unknown Confederate officer urging his men forward during the climactic charge of July 3, 1863, at Gettysburg [120]

While on the march though central Tennessee, several troops took some water out of a pond one dark night. The resulting coffee had a rich flavor. The morning light revealed dead mules in the pond! [121]

During the fighting at Perryville, Kentucky, Confederate General Ben Cheatham was urging his men forward: "Give 'em hell, boys!" His fellow general and Episcopal bishop Leonidas Polk, wishing to add to his encouragement, hollered, "Give it to 'em boys, give 'em what General Cheatham says!" [122]

A Confederate prisoner at Stone's River watched the Yankees turn and retreat into a rout. He called out, "What you running for? Why don't you stand and fight like men?" A fellow Southerner hastily shouted, "For God's sake, Joe, don't try to rally Yankees! Keep 'em on the run!" [123]

While on the march to the battle at Chickamauga, Georgia, a preacher fell in with a company of Confederates. As the troops neared battle, the preacher cried out, "Men, if any of you should die this day you will sup with the Lord tonight!" No sooner were the words out of his mouth than a cannon shot exploded overhead. The preacher whirled around on his horse and made haste towards the rear. A quick-thinking soldier hollered after the departing preacher, "Don't appear as though you is very hungry tonight Reverend!" [124]

Before the fighting erupted at Chancellorsville, the chaplains of the Federal 1st Corps held a worship service. Great appeals went up for the men to "be strong," "stand firm," "be brave," "God being a shield," "have no fear." With a sudden interruption, a Confederate shell burst over the service. However, the noise of the yells and laughter of the men at the sight of the chaplains running to the rear was louder than the artillery. "Stand firm; put your trust in the Lord!" "Come back and earn your money!"

With the fighting at an ebb, no power on heaven or earth could persuade those chaplains to venture back onto the battlefield. [125]

Father William Corby was one chaplain who shared the dangers of the battlefield with his men. On July 2, 1863, during the fierce fighting at Gettysburg, Father Corby mounted a rock and pronounced a general absolution on the men of the Irish Brigade just moments before they rushed into the caldron of battle. [126]

A member of Stonewall Jackson's commissary once remarked, "Nobody seems to understand him. But so it has been and ever will be: when we ordinary mortals can't comprehend a genius we get even with him by calling him crazy." [127]

Toward the end of the Battle of Chickamauga, an officer came upon a wounded soldier being carried off the field.

The officer called out, "Who is that?"

The answer came back, "Jimmie Rutledge, Sir."

"Who is that you have there?"

"Billy Bethune, Sir."

"Is he wounded?"

"He is sir," said Jimmie.

"How is he wounded?"

"He is shot in the back, Sir."

At that moment Billy's young voice rang out in a sharp tone of indignation, "Sir, Jimmie is a damned liar; I am shot ACROSS the back!" [128]

John B. Hood's Texans could not be faulted if they became just a bit superstitious—their commander was wounded at Gettysburg and Chickamauga while riding borrowed horses. [129]

Mary Todd Lincoln's brother-in-law, Confederate General Benjamin H. Helm, was overheard repeating the word "victory" as he lay mortally wounded at Chickamauga. [130]
(Following her husband's death, Emilie Helm was invited by her brother-in-law, President Lincoln, to relocate to Washington, D.C. and stay in the White House.)

While on the march to Gettysburg, some Federals stopped by a Dutch farm and bought some bread, apple butter, and cheese. The cheese came in balls the size of a baseball and had such an offensive odor that it proved repulsive. Since the cheese balls could not be eaten, the soldiers naturally threw them at one another, thus loosing a dense odor around their company. [131]

As the 48th Georgia moved toward a date with destiny in Gettysburg, they passed through Chambersburg to find a group of young ladies dressed in white dresses with red and blue ribbons singing "Uncle Sam's" national songs. With the playing of bands and shouts of the soldiers, it was impossible to hear what they were singing, but they sang without interruption. There was no demonstration against this effort to show the patriotism of these young ladies. [132]

On the first day of fighting in Gettysburg, as bullets whizzed in the air about him, a boy stood in the middle of Baltimore Street throwing stones at windows and laughing loudly every time he broke one. The flying bullets had no terror for him; when one came too close he would duck, laugh, and return to breaking windows. [133]

Civilians often shared their opinions with soldiers. "While we were crossing a field (outside Gettysburg), a farmer approached me, and said, 'I say mister, won't you all fight on somebody else's ground?' It was needless to say that we did not accommodate him." [134]

Overheard before Pickett's Charge, "Lord, make me a child again!"

From out of the ranks came another voice, "Yes, Lord, a gal child!" [135]

During the desperate charge of Wright's Brigade on July 2, Colorbearer Elias Denson was wounded in the thigh. Denson turned to Stephen Megahee and asked him to carry the colors forward. Stephen replied, "But who will care for my musket? I signed for it and it cost five dollars!" Denson assured the young Georgian it would be alright to leave the musket on the field. With that young Stephen grabbed the colors and rushed towards the enemy. Stephen Megahee's body was later found near the fallen colors on that blood-soaked Pennsylvania ridge. [136]

"Do your duty in all things. You cannot do more; you should never wish to do less."
—Robert E. Lee [137]

During the blockade of Vicksburg a child was born in one of the caves, and he was named William Siege Green. [138]

General Herman Haupt, Federal transportation officer, had to overcome many problems trying to operate a railroad during wartime. A continuing problem was soldiers bathing and washing clothes in water intended for the steam locomotives. As a result, said Haupt, "many engines were stopped on the road by foamy boilers caused by soapy water." [139]

At Chancellorsville, a twelve-year-old Confederate artilleryman was seen pulling the lanyard of his gun. Every time he yanked it to fire, he rolled on the ground with joy, to the delight of his older comrades. [140]

As the Federal army raced in retreat from Chickamauga, Confederate General Braxton Bragg could not be convinced that a great victory was within his grasp. One of his aides brought forth a Confederate soldier who had been captured by the Federals and escaped. The soldier supported the belief that the Federals were in wild retreat. Bragg still refused to believe it. "Do you know what a retreat looks like?" he asked. The soldier stared back and replied, "I ought to know, I've been with you during your whole campaign!" [141]

"There is a true glory and a true honor—the glory of duty done, the honor of the integrity of principle."

—Robert E. Lee [142]

As the winter of 1863 fell upon the armies in Virginia, some pickets from each side began a unique fraternization. The men came up with a great bargain. The Federals were using a deserted log hut during the day, pulling back closer to camp at night. Confederates used the hut at night, returning to their lines at daybreak. The two groups met one morning as the Confederates were slow to leave. Though everyone reached for their weapons, no one fired. Instead, they talked. An agreement was reached where Confederates would be allowed to saddle up and leave. As the men parted, someone had an afterthought. Thereafter, until fighting resumed in the spring, each group left a warm fire burning for its foe. [143]

Albert C. Lincoln, resident of the Shenandoah Valley, was less than pleased with his distant cousin who lived in Washington, D.C. Albert was heard to remark, "As long as Cousin Abe keeps sendin' 'em down the Valley, Cousin Al will keep killin' 'em." [144]

After being wounded and captured on the second day of Gettysburg, Colonel William Gibson, 48th Georgia Infantry, penned these words to his captor:

"Dear Captain: I had hoped to meet you again to express to you my thanks for the kindness and attention shown me by you on the 2d inst., yet circumstances have prevented, and I regret to learn that on the next day you were wounded, yet I am much gratified to know you are recovering, and hope you will soon be fully restored to health. I now think I shall recover myself, and trust that peace may soon be restored to our unhappy people, and that I may have an opportunity of expressing my thanks to you in a manner more agreeable and pleasant to us both. Dr. Dwinelle has done all for me that I could wish, and his kindness to me will never be forgotten. He has the will and the sense to do his whole duty to his fellow-man, and is an upright, just and honorable gentleman.

Hoping to meet soon again, as friends and brothers would meet,

I am Captain, very respectfully and truly, your obedient servant." [145]

THE THIRD YEAR OF TRIBULATION LEFT America mourning fathers, brothers, and sons lost to the "gods of war." Few stains were found on the brave men's stones, yet many cheeks were damp from tears. What had been so easy to begin was proving extremely difficult to end. The battlefields at Chancellorsville, Vicksburg, and Gettysburg were testaments to the futility of war. President Lincoln pronounced the greatest tribute to these sacrifices when he uttered the immortal words "...The brave men living and dead, who struggled here, have consecrated it, far above our poor power to add or detract...."

# 1864

THIS WAR THAT WAS SUPPOSED TO BE over in just a few months was now moving into a sea of blood and an ocean of tears. How does one stop a war? Ulysses S. Grant seemed to hold the answer. President Lincoln overlooked Grant's social concerns and raised the general's rank to commander of all Federal forces. Lincoln gave Grant one order—restore the fractured Union and do it quickly.

In Richmond, Jefferson Davis was hoping that his men, under the brilliant "Marse Robert," could hold on long enough for the Northern elections in November. Maybe a populace tired of bloodshed would deliver to the South what conflict could not bring—independence.

## TIME LINE

**2 March**      Ulysses S. Grant is promoted to Lieutenant General.

**5 May**       Battle of the Wilderness begins in Virginia.

| | |
|---|---|
| **7 May** | William T. Sherman begins his Atlanta campaign. |
| **12 May** | Battle of Spotsylvania, Virginia |
| **13 May** | Battle of Resaca, Georgia |
| **24 May** | Battle of North Anna River, Virginia. General Jeb Stuart is killed. |
| **25 May** | Battle of New Hope Church, Georgia |
| **1 June** | Battle of Cold Harbor, Virginia |
| **10 June** | Battle of Brice's Crossroads, Mississippi |
| **18 June** | Siege of Petersburg, Virginia, begins. |
| **19 June** | Naval engagement between USS *Kearsarge* and CSS *Alabama* off the coast of Cherbourg, France. |
| **17 July** | General John B. Hood replaces General Joe Johnston. Sherman threatens Atlanta. |
| **20 July** | Battle of Peachtree Creek (Atlanta), Georgia |

| | |
|---|---|
| **22 July** | Battle of Atlanta, Georgia |
| **30 July** | Battle of "the Crater" Petersburg, Virginia |
| **5 August** | Battle of Mobile Bay, Alabama |
| **1 September** | Atlanta surrenders |
| **11 September** | Civilians forced to evacuate Atlanta |
| **19 October** | Battle of Winchester, Virginia |
| **8 November** | President Lincoln is elected to second term. |
| **16 November** | William T. Sherman begins the "March to the Sea." |
| **30 November** | Battle of Franklin, Tennessee |
| **15 December** | Battle of Nashville, Tennessee |
| **21 December** | Savannah, Georgia, is occupied by Sherman's troops, ending the "March to the Sea." |

"Grant has gone to the Wilderness, crawled in, drawn up the ladder, and pulled in the hole after him, and I guess we'll have to wait till he comes out before we know just what he's up to."

—Abraham Lincoln, on hearing of Grant's determination to stay in the field after the slaughter in the Wilderness [146]

Fright could make even large men lose their composure. At six feet tall with a size thirteen shoe, Ayleshire of the 10th Virginia made a spectacle of himself at Spotsylvania. Ayleshire, known to be somewhat cowardly, slipped and slid for nearly a half-hour trying to dodge incoming shells. He had nearly worked himself to death as his comrades laughed themselves silly at his antics. John Casler later wrote of the scene, "I was wishing a shell would take his knapsack off without hurting him. If one had I believe he would have died right there from fright." [147]

Tom Jones had a bad habit of slouching while riding his horse; after a bullet passed nearby he jerked upright and ever after remained properly in the saddle. [148]

Soldiers in Tennessee had to endure not only fighting each other, but also endure fighting the elements. A staff member on General William Hardee's staff asked Hardee the derivation of the name Tullahoma, Tennessee. The general mused and looked out on the rain-drenched countryside and said it came from Greek: TULLA meaning, "mud" and HOMA meaning "more mud." [149]

"Uncle Abe was very tender hearted about shooting a deserter, but...he was perfectly willing to sacrifice a thousand brave men in a useless fight."
—Comments by Federal officer Henry Abbott [150]

"Stick to it Charlie; I've got a thirty days' furlough...."
— From a wounded Federal officer at the Wilderness [151]

In the excitement over the victory at Missionary Ridge, a Federal officer seated himself upon a recently captured cannon. The scorching barrel quickly seared the officer's bottom so that he could not sit for several days. [152]

General Lee was not alone in his concern for the common soldier. Isaac Hermann was staying the night at the home of a Mr. Rothschild. During the night Isaac, unused to the comforts of a soft bed, spent the night on the floor. Rothschild was greatly astonished at this behavior and inquired as to why Isaac preferred to sleep on the floor. Isaac replied that as he was used to hard surfaces the floor was more comfortable. [153]

Not all soldiers kept themselves presentable. Two brothers in the 39th Ohio were particularly loathsome. They became so dirty that they were not distinguishable from one another. Their comrades resorted to a forced bathing under a corporal's guard. [154]

As the Federal army moved closer to Richmond during the hot summer of 1864, a group of soldiers was ordered to bathe in the James River. The men took off their boots but remained in their clothes. They soaped up, working suds into their uniforms and their grime-encrusted skin. Floating happily in the river, they rinsed and then clambered to the bank where they dried themselves in the warm sun. When the order to resume marching was given, the men were clean and their spirits revived. [155]

Water not only cleared away the dirt as the 4th Texas crossed the Rapidan River; it also carried away a bothersome fiddle. The men slept undisturbed afterwards. [156]

On November 30, 1864, Federals preparing to assault heavy Confederate fortifications along Mine Run grimly added to their names and regiments the words "killed in action"; these slips would help to identify their remains. [157]

Grant Carter wrote to his sister of a wintertime adventure, "…We all commenced snowballing our battalion and the 3rd Georgia regiment against the 48th and 22nd Georgia regiments.…General Wright (Ambrose), his wife and daughters and other young ladies came to see the fight. We got whipped, but the ladies were the cause. The boys stopped to look at them, and the other side fought, so our party kept giving back until the others got the general and the girls prisoners.…" [158]

When General Lee granted the Federals a truce to bury their dead from the dreadful charge at Cold Harbor, the Confederates made use of the time to barter with the Federals. One Georgia private recalled, "We traded tobacco for coffee and knives. I got a little black handle, three-bladed knife, not much account. After the armistice was over we fired at each other and kept each other in the ditches very close." [159]

After the reversals in the Wilderness, General Grant was asked how long he thought it would take to get to Richmond. Grant wryly replied, "I will agree to be there in about four days, that is, if General Lee becomes party to the agreement; but if he objects, the trip will undoubtedly be prolonged." [160]

Evander Law had seen a lot of fighting, but none worse than the Federal charges against his position at Cold Harbor. Law remarked, "I had seen the dreadful carnage in front of Mayre's Hill at Fredericksburg, and on the old 'railroad cut' which Jackson's men held at the Second Manassas; but I had seen nothing to exceed this. It was not war; it was murder." [161]

The slaughter of Federals at Cold Harbor so overwhelmed Colonel Charles Venable of Lee's staff that he exclaimed the engagement was "perhaps the easiest victory ever granted to the Confederate arms by the folly of the Federal's commanders." [162]

Charles Venable's commentary on the futility of the Federal charge was echoed in the Federal ranks. Thomas Barker of the 12th New Hampshire shouted, "I will not take my regiment in another such charge if Jesus Christ himself should order it!" [163]

Colonel William Oates remarked in a letter that the final irony of Cold Harbor was that after three days in the hot sun the Federal dead gave off a terrible stench. Fortunately for the Confederates, the wind carried the odor back to the Federal lines. [164]

Brigadier General William Bartlett had his leg crushed by a Confederate shell as he led his men forward during the Battle of the Crater. The Confederate who came to escort Bartlett to the rear was astonished that Bartlett showed no sign of pain and remarked to the general that he must have nerves of steel. Bartlett replied it did not hurt to have a cork leg crushed. He had lost his leg originally at Yorktown two years earlier. [165]

"Our hard tack was very hard. We could scarcely break them with our teeth. Some we could scarcely fracture with our fist...It required some experience and no little hunger to enable one to appreciate hard tack rightly...."
    —Private William, Bircher 2nd Minnesota [166]

A rather hungry soldier was walking through shell-torn Atlanta. He was "enjoying" a piece of hard tack when a voice from above said: "Give poor Polly a cracker!" The soldier, unnerved, looked around, when again the voice called out for food. With that the soldier cried out "Gee Whilkens, boys, damned if the world hain't coming to an end. Even the birds are talking and begging for bread." Looking at the parrot, he continued, "…I'm sorry you…This is the first cracker I've seen for two days!" [167]

While awaiting the command to advance before Franklin, Tennessee, General Patrick Cleburne was observed to mark out some squares in the soft earth and began a game of checkers using colored leaves for the pieces. [168]

Both combatant armies resorted to dirt weapons at Franklin. Confederate troops hurled dirt to blind the Federals, and the Yankee troops threw dirt clods when they ran low on ammunition. [169]

Trench life was agonizing for soldiers on both sides. A Confederate was heard to mutter as he slogged through the mud, "This knocks the poetry out of war, don't it?" [170]

When the 123rd New York was posted to Chattanooga after several years in the Army of the Potomac, the New Yorkers were amazed at the relaxed atmosphere exhibited by the western soldiers. In return the western troops responded with, "Oh look at their little caps. Where are your paper collars? Oh how clean you look, do you have soap?" As the war ground on, though, the two groups become great friends and fighting partners. [171]

Richmond society would come down to Petersburg for glimpses of the enemy. The unwritten rule was that no shooting would be permitted when ladies were present. When the Yanks saw women on the earthworks, the cry would go out, "Hello, Johnnie! It's ladies' day, ain't it?" and the shooting would cease until the ladies were gone. [172]

"When we weren't killing each other, we were the best of friends."
> — The recollection of a Federal who served at Petersburg [173]

"Hello, Yanks, what's the matter with you over there?"

"We're out of wood."

"If you wanted wood why didn't you say so? We have more than we need out here, and if you had only asked us you might have sent out your teams and got all the wood you wanted without kicking up such a hell of a fuss about it."

> —Conversation between the skirmish lines after the fighting at Missionary Ridge, Tennessee, in 1864 [174]

By 1864 not many troops were happy to see their legislators. The officers and men of a Florida brigade had a great laugh when their state congressman dodged at every shot they heard, while in the meantime nearby soldiers picked flowers and went about their business. Such was life in the Petersburg trenches. [175]

When the Army of Northern Virginia came rushing into Petersburg, a woman and child stood intently watching the passing troops. Suddenly the woman sprang into the marching line and embraced a soldier around the neck and held on for dear life. How she knew who it was she hugged was a minor miracle, for all the men were dirty beyond measure. Yet she and the child, who now cried with delight, knew it was their husband and father, one who had been absent from home for two years. Many an eye in those dirty ranks shed tears as they beheld the tender scene. [176]

"Yankee armies are seldom caught when they start on a retreat. In that branch of tactics they generally excel."

> —The words of a Confederate officer as Early's men chased General Hunter through the Shenandoah Valley in 1864 [177]

During the struggle at Gravelly Road, Virginia, Joshua Lawrence Chamberlain was badly wounded. The next shell hit his horse. The wounds resulted in, as Chamberlain later vividly described, "a blood relationship of which I was not ashamed."

Nevertheless, horse and rider continued to ride toward their foe. [178]

From a letter home:
"dear wife and children
... i hope this will come safe to hand and find you all well ...we have bin fighting near Maryiter for more than a week ther has bin a grat many kild on both sides... i want to see you and the children the worst i ever did in my life...." [179]

During the Battle of New Hope Church, the exposed Confederate batteries suffered tremendously. Three brothers from Louisiana manned one gun. The oldest was the rammer and he went down with a fatal wound. The second brother took his place only to be taken down, too. With that the third brother continued to service the piece until he, as well, suffered a mortal wound. [180]

Before reaching Atlanta a soldier from the 104th Illinois called out to his Confederate counterpart: "Hello, Johnny, how far is it to Atlanta?" "So damn far you'll never get there." "Yes, we will get there, and we'll have a dance with your sister!" With that, a shower of Confederate bullets put an end to the conversation. [181]

The fighting at Kennesaw was so fierce and raw that Sam Watkins remembered his musket becoming so hot the powder would flash before he could ram home the ball. [182]

William Sherman's oft-repeated quote "war is hell" was borne out when his artillery began to shell Atlanta. The first shell arched over the city and fell at the intersection of Ivy and Ellis streets where a young girl was walking her dog. Both were killed instantly, becoming Atlanta's first casualties. [183]

One evening outside Atlanta, a Federal picket called out to the Confederates across the way: "Well, Johnny, how many of you are left?" "Oh, about enough for another killing!" came the response. [184]

As the armies dug in for a siege around Atlanta, the common soldiers fraternized frequently. Southerners traded tobacco for Northern coffee, and opposing soldiers often picked blackberries from the same bushes. At night they would duel with songs, the Federals with "Yankee Doodle," the Rebs with "Dixie," both sides joining in closing with "Home, Sweet Home." [185]

Not all officers were respected by their troops. Francis Blair, commanding Sherman's XVII Corps, herded his men on unnecessarily long marches. On the road his men would loudly bleat, "Blaa-aa-ir! Blaa-aa-ir!" [186]

Throughout Sherman's time in Georgia, his men would look for freshly buried goods and valuables. The men of the 2nd Minnesota were quite pleased when a ramrod, thrust into a fresh pile of earth, thumped on something solid. The men quickly dug up the box and just as quickly backed away as the stench of a dead dog filled their noses. "It looks like poor Curly will get no peace," the woman of the house exclaimed, "that's the fourth time he's been dug up today." [187]

General Patrick Cleburne was most likely the best-loved general in the Army of Tennessee. During the campaign for Atlanta, General Cleburne was out checking the line when he came upon a company of men who were busily cooking beef. With no time to hide their plunder, one of the men stepped to the road, saluted, and said, "General, we have some nice, fat beef cooking, and it is about done, come eat dinner with us." "Well," the General replied, "it does smell good. I reckon I'll have some." The General sat down with the men. One proceeded to fetch a piece of beef, while another found a piece of corn pone. The General ate, thanked the men for the meal, took out his pipe and began to smoke, chatting with the men, inquiring of their families and such. When Cleburne finally rose to leave, the whole company cheered him. [188]

General William Tecumseh Sherman was noted for his abruptness. However, he met his match in one volunteer nurse. As Sherman was preparing for his advance into Georgia, he ordered that only military equipment be moved into Chattanooga. This disrupted the plans of Mother Mary Ann Bickerdyke. As a leading nurse and sanitary commissioner, Mother Bickerdyke was most unhappy with the loss of transportation to the front. She bustled past Sherman's aides and confronted the General.

"You must change the order, General," she said.

"Well, I'm busy today," replied the general.

"No, fix this thing as it ought to be fixed. Have some sense about it."

Sherman tried to joke with her.

"Well, I can't stand here fooling around all day," she said. "Write an order for two cars a day!"

Sherman did as she said. When his officers complained about Mother Bickerdyke, Sherman threw up his hands and said, "She ranks me. I can't do a thing in the world." [189]

As the Battle of Dug Gap, Georgia, raged, Confederate Generals Patrick Cleburne and William Hardee rode forward to check on the progress of the fight. A brigade of Texans was ordered up from the reserves. The first Texan to reach the generals dismounted, saluted with a flourish, and asked, "Where am I most needed?" The two generals looked at the boy in disbelief and then burst into laughter. [190]

A young officer, in his efforts to construct the "Swamp Angel" battery outside Charleston, sent in a request for "...one hundred men eighteen feet high to wade through mud sixteen feet deep." This request was not found to be humorous by the commanding officer, and the young lieutenant built the fortifications with ordinary men. [191]

Shortly before the Battle of Resaca, Georgia's Confederate General John Bell Hood confided his wish to be baptized into the Episcopal Church. No problem: The fighting bishop, General Leonidas Polk, performed the service with the crippled Hood standing on his crutch and Polk using a horse bucket for the consecrated water. [192]

William Tecumseh Sherman could work long hours overseeing his army. Three to four hours sleep was all he required, with an occasional nap thrown in. Once, while Sherman was catnapping by the roadside, the following scene took place. A soldier passing by saw the sleeping form. "Is that a general?" "Yes." "A pretty way we're commanded when our general is lying drunk beside the road!"

"Stop, my man!" cried Sherman. "I'm not drunk. While YOU were sleeping last night, I was planning for you, sir! I was taking a nap." [193]

During the Battle of Kennesaw Mountain, Georgia, an unlikely truce took place. Lt. Colonel William Martin, commander of the 1st and 15th Arkansas, saw that flames were roasting many Federal wounded. Placing his handkerchief on a ramrod, Martin jumped onto the parapet to offer a truce. "Come and remove your wounded; they are burning to death, we won't fire a gun until you get them away. Be quick!"

Then, while gunfire raged over the rest of the battlefield, a merciful quiet came over this little part of the mountain. Men in gray helped men in blue to save the wounded.

After the burned area was cleared and the fire put out, a Federal major brought Colonel Martin a gift of appreciation—matched Colt revolvers. And then both sides went back to killing each other! [194]

To encourage his men during the ferocious fighting at Kennesaw, Ohio, Colonel Dan McCook recited the stanzas from Macaulay's *Horatius:*

"Then out spoke brave Horatius,
The Captain of the Gate:
To every man upon this earth
Death cometh soon or late.
And how can man die better
Than facing fearful odds,
For the ashes of his fathers,
And the temples of Gods?"

Colonel McCook later fell with a mortal wound upon the bloody ground of Kennesaw. [195]

"If it were God's will, I should like to live longer and serve my country. If I must die, I should like to see my wife first; but if it is His will that I die now, I am ready and willing to go if God and my country think that I have fulfilled my destiny and done my duty."

    — the words of James Ewell Brown Stuart, as he lay dying [196]

To cross the Chattahoochee River, some members of the Federal cavalry used a novel approach—removing their clothes before crossing the river. The first Confederate to surrender when the Federals reached the south side of the river expressed his wonderment at the methods thusly:

"I surrender, but dog-gone my skin, Yanks, 'taint fair to come at us in that way. If we'uns had been strong enough to take you'uns, the Confederate government 'ud hung all for spies, as you hain't got no uniforms on!" [197]

During the war, the Northern public became concerned over the large number of brevet, or honorary, promotions being handed out. When a wagon train of mules panicked and raced towards the enemy, spreading confusion amongst those ranks, General U. S. Grant became greatly amused. After the scene he wrote the following order, "I respectfully request that the mules, for their gallantry in this action, may have conferred upon them the brevet rank of horses." [198]

While inspecting his lines near Chattanooga, General Grant stumbled upon the fraternization common between enemy lines. As Grant approached, a Federal guard called out, "Turn out for commanding general." Not wanting to attract attention, Grant quickly replied, "Never mind." At the same moment, there came a call from across the lines, "Turn out for the commanding general," and Grant thought he heard his own name mentioned. The Confederates quickly lined up and as Grant recalled, "...fronted to the north, facing me and gave me a salute, which I returned." [199]

Rocks were used in any number of battles when ammunition ran short. George Bailie of the 63rd Georgia copied the David vs. Goliath method during the fight at Kennesaw. Picking up a stone, he threw it and hit his adversary square in the face, rendering him *hors de combat*. [200]

While General Grant was filling his army with the garrison troops from Washington and other former noncombatants, a wagon master was overheard shouting at a braying mule, "You needn't laugh at me, you may be in the ranks before Grant gets through with the Army." [201]

James Paul Verdery wrote home in February 1864 of his encounter with "Marse" Robert E. Lee:

"I had taken my seat in the church. To my great surprise and enthusiasm our commander in chief of Confederate Army Gen. R. E. Lee came and seats himself directly in the seat right in front of me. You can well imagine that I feel highly honored by being so near him. His looks remind me a great deal of father, he is without any exception the best looking old man I ever saw. I think father will take this as a compliment...." [202]

BOTH SIDES WERE IN AGREEMENT AFTER the fourth year of fighting—the war had long since lost its "poetry!" The experiences in Georgia and in the trenches around Petersburg sapped even the strongest of hearts. Yet it would be stout hearts that would see the nation through to the end. The coming of spring would see dramatic changes and a chance for new beginnings.

# 1865

THE AIR WAS LADEN ONCE AGAIN WITH honeysuckle and magnolias. After four years of war, the coming of spring meant only one thing to Americans hardened by war: armies would be on the move, lives were about to change forever.

## TIME LINE

| | |
|---|---|
| **15 January** | Fort Fisher at Wilmington, North Carolina, falls, leaving the Confederacy with no open seaports. |
| **19 January** | Robert E. Lee appointed general-in-chief of all Confederate forces. |
| **1 February** | William T. Sherman's troops cross into South Carolina. |
| **3 February** | President Lincoln meets with Confederate vice-president Alexander Stephens to discuss peace terms. The meeting is unsuccessful. |

| | |
|---|---|
| **17 February** | Columbia, South Carolina, falls to Sherman's troops; most of the city is burned. |
| **4 March** | President Lincoln is inaugurated to his second term. |
| **21 March** | Battle of Bentonville, North Carolina |
| **25 March** | Battle of Fort Steadman, Virginia |
| **27 March** | President Lincoln confers with Generals Grant, Sherman, and Admiral Porter at City Point, Virginia, regarding war plans. |
| **1 April** | Battle of Five Forks, Virginia |
| **2 April** | Richmond evacuated; Confederate President Jefferson Davis flees south. |
| **3 April** | Richmond surrenders to Federal forces. |
| **4 April** | President Lincoln tours Richmond. |
| **6 April** | Battle of Sayler's Creek, Virginia |

| | |
|---|---|
| **7 April** | General Grant inquires about General Lee's intentions regarding the surrender of the Confederate army. |
| **9 April** | General Lee accepts Grant's terms of surrender at Appomattox Court House, Virginia. |
| **12 April** | Army of Northern Virginia formally surrenders. |
| **14 April** | President Lincoln is assassinated while attending Ford's Theater in Washington, D.C. |
| **18 April** | General Joe Johnston discusses surrender terms with General William T. Sherman in Durham, North Carolina. |
| **26 April** | John Wilkes Booth, the accused assassin of President Lincoln, is shot and killed.

Joe Johnston surrenders the Army of Tennessee. |

**10 May**          Confederate President Jefferson Davis
                    is captured in Irwinville, Georgia.

**23 May**          Grand parade of the Federal armies
                    in Washington, D.C.

**August 1866**     President Andrew Johnson proclaims,
                    "…said insurrection is at an end."

"I would rather die then to have anyone say I shirked duty."

—R. L. Phillips, Weisiger's Virginia Brigade [203]

It was very near the end of the war. A weary and bedraggled Confederate sat cooling his feet in a stream and mending his threadbare clothing. Suddenly he was accosted by a Federal who shouted, "Hey, Johnny, I've got you this time."

Without looking up the Confederate replied, "Yes, and a hell of a git you got!" [204]

As Ambrose Burnside watched his soldiers marching through a small Virginia town, he remarked to a woman nearby, "I don't suppose, madam, that you ever saw so many Yankee soldiers before." Her reply: "Not at liberty, sir!" [205]

Two young Virginia Military Institute cadets were straggling along the Valley turnpike. When two horsemen rode by, the boys begged one for a ride. One cadet asked: "Mister, won't you take me up behind?"

As they rode along, the cadet asked, "What cavalry company do you belong to?"

"I don't belong to any," came the answer.

"Well, to what battery?"

"To none."

"Well to what regiment then?"

"To none—I am General Winder of the Stonewall Brigade."

"Oh! General!" gasped the cadet, "I beg your pardon, I never would have asked you to take me up if I had known who you were!"

The cadet made motions to slide off, but General Winder insisted the boy remain and carried him a good ways up the Valley. [206]

General Lee had a very kind and understanding manner in dealing with his subordinates. When A. P. Hill became enraged with Ambrose Wright after Spotsylvania, Lee suggested the following:

"These men are not an army; they are citizens defending their country. General Wright is not a soldier; he is a lawyer....if you humiliate General Wright, the people of Georgia would not understand. When a man makes a mistake, I call him into my tent, and use the authority of my position to make him do the right thing the next time." [207]

Following the surrender at Appomattox, General Fitzhugh Lee rode towards Richmond and home. While riding he met up with an old soldier.

"Ho, there," cried out Fitzhugh, "where are you going?"

"I've been on furlough, and am going back to join Marse Robert," said the soldier.

"You needn't go back, for Lee has surrendered," said the general. "Go to your home."

"Lee surrendered?"

"That's what I said," replied the general.

"It must have been that damned Fitz Lee then, Marse Robert would never surrender," replied the soldier.

With that the old soldier put on a look of disgust and walked on. [208]

Jefferson Davis bore the weight of the war with a concern only matched by that of Abraham Lincoln. Both men lost children during the war. Davis's son Joe fell from the porch at the Confederate White House. Lincoln's energetic son Tad died from fever. [209]

General Wade Hampton's Confederate cavalry pulled off a neat trick and hijacked a herd of beef intended for the Federals. Shortly thereafter, Ulysses Grant was asked how long before the Federals would be in Richmond. Grant replied, "Never, if our armies continue to supply him (Lee) with beef-cattle." [210]

General Wade Hampton's son Preston was mortally wounded at Hatcher's Run. General Hampton arrived by his son's side and wept as he realized his son was fading quickly. Waving the surgeon away Hampton cried, "Too late, doctor, too late." With that Hampton mounted and returned to the fight. [211]

The war dragged on, and both the Blue and the Gray could agree with the words of Henry Greer, 25th South Carolina: "I think of all things in this world, I hate war and the army the worst, but I am here and here I will have to stay." [212]

"Jubal Early's men stopped during the pursuit of the enemy to honor their deceased commander and hero, Stonewall Jackson. They marched through the cemetery—men in two ranks at reverse arms in column, the officers on foot, and when they passed the tomb they uncovered [removed their hats]." [213]

—Captain Cary Whitaker, Company D, 43rd North Carolina Infantry

During the siege of Petersburg, a group of lovely young ladies called upon General Lee. They wanted his judgment about parties and dance during the difficult times. General Lee's response: "Why, of course. My boys need to be heartened up when they get their furloughs. Go on, look your prettiest, and be just as nice to them as ever you can be!" [214]

April 2, 1865, the day Petersburg fell, was not the time to ask for time off to be married, but that is what Colonel Walter Taylor asked of General Lee. The General's reply: "My congratulations to the bride." [215]

As Robert E. Lee was making final preparation to break through the surrounding Federal army near Appomattox, General John Gordon inquired as to how far he (Gordon) should advance if he were able to break the Federal lines. General Lee replied, "...halt just beyond the Tennessee line." (Tennessee was 200 miles away.) [216]

The Rev. Dr. Charles Minegerode, the rector of St. Paul's Church in Richmond, had just delivered an invitation for the congregation to come forward to receive the consecrated bread and wine, when a tall, well-dressed, black man stood and walked to the rail. There followed a very definite pause in the church. The congregation appeared deeply chagrined at this attempt to offend and humiliate them, and the good Rev. Dr. Minegerode was very embarrassed. Then another person rose from a pew and walked down the aisle to the chancel rail. He knelt by the black man and so redeemed the situation. The second gentleman was Robert E. Lee. [217]

"A true gentleman of honor feels humbled himself when he cannot help humbling others."
—Robert E. Lee [218]

During Robert E. Lee's tenure at Washington College, he encountered a student who was overworking himself. Lee advised the student to ease up, to which the student replied, "I am so impatient to make up for the time I was in the army."

Lee turned a deep red and responded, "However long you live and whatever you accomplish, you will find that the time you spent in the Confederate Army was the most profitably spent portion of your life. Never again speak of having lost time in the army!" [219]

Overheard during Robert E. Lee's trip through the South in 1870: "We regarded him with the greatest veneration. We had heard of God, but here was General Lee." [220]

A Confederate soldier devised a plan for survival. "I always shot at privates. It was they that did the shooting and killing, and if I could kill or wound a private, why my chances were so much better. I always looked upon officers as harmless personages." [221]

Federal soldiers who were fortunate to carry seven-shot Spencer repeating rifles held them in high regard. One fatally wounded soldier lacked the strength to smash his piece so he took out his knife, unscrewed the lock plate, and threw it as far as he could, rendering the gun useless. Then he rolled over and died. [222]

Sherman's army was a mix of eastern and western soldiers. At times there was friction between the troops, but beneath the regional differences lay a unity of purpose. A solider on the march put it quite properly: When asked to which corps he belonged, he sharply replied, "Corps? What do you mean, 'corps?' I belong to General Sherman's army!" [223]

While Sherman marched through and terrorized South Carolina, a squad of Yankees had their comeuppance at the hands of Mother Nature. It seems that while a squad of Yankees were ransacking a farmhouse, some men went for the beehive in the backyard. The farmer's young daughter protested the fact that the Yankees were about to steal the honey, when a swarm of bees "fixed bayonets" and presently had the Yankees on the run. The young girl would later recall how much fun she had watching her Southern bees rout the Yankees right off her daddy's farm. The Yankees dropped all the plunder in their haste to get away from the bees. [224]

As Sherman moved his Union troops into South Carolina, his army had to cross numerous swamps. The troops became quite proficient in building corduroy roads. This technique so impressed the Confederates that one tired Southern prisoner was heard to remark that if Sherman's men were sent to hell "they'd corduroy it and march on it." [225]

"Thank God I have a backbone for my stomach to lean up against."

—Comment made by a hungry Confederate in 1865 [226]

Overheard in the trenches of Petersburg: "My shoes are gone. I'm sick. I'm hungry. My family have been killed or scattered. I have suffered all this for my country. I love my country. I would die—yes, I would die willingly because I love my country. But if this war is ever over, I'll be damned if I ever love another country!" [227]

On New Year's Day of 1865, the women of Richmond promised to bring the army a feast. All day the men in the trenches waited for the food to arrive. Some even refused to eat their regular fare in order to enjoy the promised repast. Sometime after midnight the men received the food sent by the devoted ladies: two tiny slices of bread and a thin piece of ham. As the men ate their food, which was better than the normal rations, one man was heard to remark, "God bless our noble women, it was all they could do; it was all they had." [228]

General Braxton Bragg was not well liked by his men. While traveling down a Tennessee road one afternoon, Bragg and his staff came upon a lone soldier and the following conversation took place.

"Who are you?" asked Bragg.

"Nobody," came the reply.

"Where did you come from?"

"Nowhere."

"Where are you going?"

"I don't know."

"Where do you belong?"

"Don't belong nowhere."

"Don't you belong to Bragg's army?"

"Bragg's army! Bragg's army? Why he's ain't got no army. One half he shot in Kentucky and the other half just bin whipped to death at Murfreesboro!"

General Bragg rode off without another word. [229]

"Why, sir, in the beginning we appointed all our worst generals to command the armies, and all our best generals to edit the newspapers. As you know, I planned some campaigns and quite a number of battles. I have given the work all the care and thought I could, and sometimes, when my plans were completed, as far as I could see they seemed to be perfect. But when I have fought them through I have discovered defects, and occasionally wondered why I did not see some of the defects in advance. When it was all over, I found by reading a newspaper that these best editor-generals saw all the defects plainly from the start. Unfortunately, they did not communicate their knowledge to me until it was too late."

—Robert E. Lee in the spring of 1865 [230]

"My very dear Sarah:

The indications are very strong that we shall move in a few days, perhaps tomorrow. Lest I should not be able to write again, I feel impelled to write a few lines that may fall under your eye when I shall be no more... 'Not my will but Thine, O God be done.' If it is necessary that I should fall on the battlefield for my Country, I am ready....

Sarah, my love for you is deathless... Sullivan"

(Major Sullivan Ballou fell at First Bull Run) [231]

THIS TERRIBLE WAR PRODUCED MANY stories. It also produced two documents that provided a basis for the rebirth of our nation: Robert E. Lee's farewell Order Number Nine and Abraham Lincoln's words at Gettysburg.

# Order Number Nine

"After four years of arduous service marked by unsurpassed courage and fortitude, the Army of Northern Virginia has been compelled to yield to overwhelming numbers and resources.

I need not tell the brave survivors of so many hard fought battles, who have remained steadfast to the last, that I have consented to this result from no distrust of them. But feeling that valor and devotion could accomplish nothing that could compensate for the loss that must have attended the continuance of the contest, I determined to avoid the useless sacrifice of those whose past services have endeared them to their countrymen.

By terms of the agreement officers and men can return to their homes and remain until exchanged. You will take with you the satisfaction that proceeds from the consciousness of duty faithfully performed, and I earnestly pray that a merciful God will extend to you His blessings and protection.

With an increasing admiration of your constancy and devotion to your country, and a grateful remembrance of your kind and generous consideration for myself, I bid you all an affectionate farewell."

—Robert E. Lee, April 10, 1865
Appomattox, Virginia

# The Gettysburg Address

"Four score and seven years ago our fathers brought forth upon this continent a new nation, conceived in liberty, and dedicated to the proposition that all men are created equal.

Now we are engaged in a great civil war, testing whether that nation, or any nation so conceived and so dedicated, can long endure. We are met on a great battlefield of that war. We have come to dedicate a portion of that field as a final resting-place of those who here gave their lives that that nation might live. It is altogether fitting and proper that we should do this.

But in a larger sense we cannot dedicate, we cannot consecrate, we cannot hallow this ground. The brave men, living and dead, who struggled here, have consecrated it far above our poor power to add or detract. The world will little note, nor long remember, what we say here, but it can never forget what they did here. It is for us, the living, rather to be dedicated here to the unfinished work they have thus far so nobly advanced. It is rather for us to be here dedicated to the great task remaining before us, that from these honored dead we take increased devotion to that cause for which they here gave the last full measure of devotion; that we here highly resolve that the dead shall not have died in vain, that this nation, under God, shall have a new birth of freedom; and that government of the people, by the people, and for the people, shall not perish from the earth."

—Abraham Lincoln, November 19, 1863
Gettysburg, Pennsylvania

# ENDNOTES

## 1861

1. Robertson, *Stonewall Jackson*: 210.
2. Davis, *First Blood*: 14.
3. Time Life Books, *Soldier Life—Voices*: 11.
4. Time Life Books, *Soldier Life—Voices*: 12.
5. Davis, *First Blood*: 116.
6. Davis, *First Blood*: 116.
7. Hassler, *Colonel John Pelham*: 19.
8. Botkin, *A Civil War Treasury*: 50-51.
9. Robertson, *Stonewall Jackson*: 267.
10. Davis, *First Blood*: 155.
11. Robertson, *Stonewall Jackson*: 271.
12. Watkins, *CO. Aytch*: 46.
13. Robertson, *Stonewall Jackson*: 483.
14. Bailey, *Forward to Richmond*: 31.
15. Nevin, *The Road to Shiloh*: 21.
16. Bailey, *Forward to Richmond*: 42.
17. Time Life Books, *Spies, Scouts and Raiders*: 8.
18. Bailey, *Forward to Richmond*: 78.
19. Bailey, *Forward to Richmond*: 99.
20. Robertson, *Stonewall Jackson*: 241.
21. Time Life Books, *Soldier Life—Voices*: 36.
22. Watkins, *CO. Aytch*: 26.
23. Watkins, *CO. Aytch*: 30.
24. Gowan, *Stories, Anecdotes and Humor from the Civil War*: 2.
25. Gowan, *Stories, Anecdotes and Humor from the Civil War*: 8.
26. Gowan, *Stories, Anecdotes and Humor from the Civil War*: 9.
27. Gowan, *Stories, Anecdotes and Humor from the Civil War*: 12-13.
28. Burns, *The Civil War*: film commentary by Shelby Foote.
29. Botkin, *A Civil War Treasury*: 111-112.
30. Rhodes, *All for the Union*: 50.
31. Robertson, *Tenting Tonight*: 59.
32. Time Life Books, *Soldier Life—Voices*: 82.

33. Rhodes, *All for the Union*: 167.
34. Burns, *The Civil War*: film commentary by Shelby Foote.

**1862**

35. Botkin, *A Civil War Treasury*: 83.
36. Botkin, *A Civil War Treasury*: 27-28.
37. Bailey, *Forward to Richmond*: 99.
38. Bailey, *Forward to Richmond*: 105.
39. Bailey, *Forward to Richmond*: 138.
40. Nevin, *The Road to Shiloh*: 106-107.
41. Bailey, *Forward to Richmond*: 93.
42. Channing, *Confederate Ordeal*: 59.
43. Time Life Books, *Lee Takes Command*: 60.
44. Botkin, *A Civil War Treasury*: 61-63.
45. Time Life Books, *The Blockade*: 67.
46. Bailey, *Forward to Richmond*: 110.
47. Bailey, *Forward to Richmond*: 156.
48. Bailey, *Forward to Richmond*: 160.
49. Bailey, *Forward to Richmond*: 161.
50. Time Life Books, *Lee Takes Command*: 8.
51. Time Life Books, *Lee Takes Command*: 65.
52. Time Life Books, *Lee Takes Command*: 95.
53. Time Life Books, *Antietam—Voices*: 155.
54. Time Life Books, *Shiloh—Voices*: 112.
55. Street, *The Struggle for Tennessee*: 49.
56. Street, *The Struggle for Tennessee*: 58.
57. Street, *The Struggle for Tennessee*: 66-67.
58. Botkin, *A Civil War Treasury*: 225-226.
59. Time Life Books, *Lee Takes Command*: 158.
60. Time Life Books, *Second Manassas—Voices*: 30.
61. Jackson, *Twenty Million Yankees*: 125.
62. Time Life Books, *Second Manassas—Voices*: 103.
63. Time Life Books, *Second Manassas—Voices*: 110.
64. Time Life Books, *Antietam—Voices*: 104.

65. Time Life Books, *Second Manassas—Voices*: 139.
66. Sears, *Landscape Turned Red*: 71.
67. Robertson, *Stonewall Jackson*: xiv.
68. Time Life Books, *Antietam—Voices*: 25.
69. Time Life Books, *Antietam—Voices*: 25.
70. Time Life Books, *Antietam—Voices*: 36.
71. Bailey, *Bloodiest Day*: 54.
72. Bailey, *Bloodiest Day*: 70.
73. Goolrich, *Rebels Resurgent*: 33.
74. Time Life Books, *Shenandoah 1862—Voices*: 25.
75. Goolrich, *Rebels Resurgent*: 41.
76. Robertson, *Stonewall Jackson*: 456.
77. Time Life Books, *Soldier Life—Voices*: 39.
78. Watkins, *CO. Aytch*: 36.
79. Time Life Books, *Antietam—Voices*: 136.
80. Rhodes, *All for the Union*: 103-104.
81. Bailey, *Rebels Resurgent*: 77.
82. Bedwell, *May I Quote You General Lee?*: 24.
83. Jaynes, *The Killing Ground*: 33-34
84. Nevin, *The Road to Shiloh*: 65.
85. Time Life Books, *Vicksburg—Voices*: 75.
86. Nevin, *The Road to Shiloh*: 122.
87. Bailey, *Bloodiest Day*: 13.
88. Bailey, *Bloodiest Day*: 102.
89. Bailey, *Bloodiest Day*: 103.
90. Street, *The Struggle for Tennessee*: 118.
91. Street, *The Struggle for Tennessee*: 121.

**1863**

92. Time Life Books, *Lee Takes Command*: 106-107
93. Robertson, *Stonewall Jackson*: xiv.
94. Time Life Books, *Chancellorsville—Voices*: 116.
95. Bailey, *Bloodiest Day*: 15.
96. Time Life Books, *Spies, Scouts and Raiders*: 119.
97. Bailey, *Bloodiest Day*: 19.
98. Time Life Books, *Wilderness—Voices*: 19.

99. Bailey, *Bloodiest Day*: 21.
100. Time Life Books, *Lee Takes Command*: 125.
101. Robertson, *Stonewall Jackson*: 342.
102. Time Life Books, *Shenandoah 1862—Voices*: 22.
103. Robertson, *Stonewall Jackson*: x.
104. Goolrich, *Rebels Resurgent*: 34.
105. Robertson, *Stonewall Jackson*: x.
106. Goolrich, *Rebels Resurgent*: 38.
107. Time Life Books, *Soldier Life—Voices*: 121.
108. Goolrich, *Rebels Resurgent*: 146.
109. Clark, *Gettysburg*: 14.
110. Time Life Books, *Soldier Life—Voices*: 122.
111. Clark, *Gettysburg*: 34.
112. Clark, *Gettysburg*: 59.
113. Clark, *Gettysburg*: 67.
114. Time Life Books, *Gettysburg—Voices*: 115.
115. Botkin: *A Civil War Treasury*: 266.
116. Time Life Books, *Chancellorsville—Voices*: 20.
117. Time Life Books, *Chancellorsville—Voices*: 56.
118. Joslyn, *A Meteor Shining Brightly*: 102.
119. Time Life Books, *Shiloh—Voices*: 158.
120. Clark, *Gettysburg*: 138.
121. Street, *The Struggle for Tennessee*: 58.
122. Street, *The Struggle for Tennessee*: 64.
123. Street, *The Struggle for Tennessee*: 117.
124. Watkins, *CO. Aytch*: 91.
125. Time Life Books, *Chancellorsville—Voices*: 54.
126. Clark, *Gettysburg*: 100.
127. Robertson, *Stonewall Jackson*: xi.
128. Botkin, *A Civil War Treasury*: 338.
129. Korn, *The Fight for Chattanooga*: 60.
130. Korn, *The Fight for Chattanooga*: 62. Caroli, *Inside The White House*: 26.
131. Pfanz, *Gettysburg—Culp's Hill & Cemetery Hill*: 143.
132. Zwemer, *For Home and the Southland*: 28.
133. Pfanz, *Gettysburg—Culp's Hill & Cemetery Hill*: 92.
134. *Gettysburg Magazine* #21: 65.

135. Shaara, *The Killer Angels*: 317.
136. Zwemer, *For Home and the Southland*: xx.
137. Thomas, *Robert E. Lee*: 397.
138. Time Life Books, *Vicksburg—Voices*: 113.
139. Goolrich, *Rebels Resurgent*: 21.
140. Goolrich, *Rebels Resurgent*: 147
141. Korn, *The Fight for Chattanooga*: 72.
142. Time Life Books, *Lee Takes Command*: 8.
143. Robertson, *Tenting Tonight*: 158.
144. Time Life Books, *Shenandoah 1862—Voices*: 126.
145. Zwemer, *For Home and the Southland*: 36.

## 1864

146. Time Life Books, *Wilderness—Voices*: 113.
147. Time Life Books, *Wilderness—Voices*: 115.
148. Time Life Books, *Wilderness—Voices*: 127.
149. Korn, *The Fight for Chattanooga*: 29.
150. Time Life Books, *Wilderness—Voices*: 17.
151. Time Life Books, *Wilderness—Voices*: 57.
152. Korn, *The Fight for Chattanooga*: 149.
153. Time Life Books, *Soldier Life—Voices*: 133.
154. Time Life Books, *Soldier Life—Voices*: 91.
155. Trulock, *In the Hands of Providence*: 195.
156. Time Life Books, *Soldier Life—Voices*: 49.
157. Jaynes, *The Killing Ground*: 31.
158. Zwemer, *For Home and the Southland*: 28.
159. Power, *Lee's Miserables*: 66.
160. Jaynes, *The Killing Ground*: 60.
161. Jaynes, *The Killing Ground*: 158.
162. Jaynes, *The Killing Ground*: 165.
163. Jaynes, *The Killing Ground*: 166.
164. Jaynes, *The Killing Ground*: 167.
165. Davis, *Death in the Trenches*: 68.
166. Time Life Books, *Soldier Life—Voices*: 96-97.
167. Time Life Books, *Soldier Life—Voices*: 107.
168. Nevin, *Sherman's March*: 102.

169. Nevin, *Sherman's March*: 115.

170. Davis, *Death in the Trenches*: 136.

171. Time Life Books, *Chattanooga—Voices*: 76.

172. Davis, *Death in the Trenches*: 137.

173. Davis, *Death in the Trenches*: 159.

174. Time Life Books, *Chattanooga—Voices*: 87.

175. Power, *Lee's Miserables*: 72.

176. Power, *Lee's Miserables*: 87.

177. Power, *Lee's Miserables*: 91.

178. Korn, *Pursuit to Appomattox*: 81.

179. Gragg, *The Illustrated Confederate Reader*: 66.

180. Bailey, *Battles for Atlanta*: 52.

181. Bailey, *Battles for Atlanta*: 60.

182. Watkins, *CO. Aytch*: 150.

183. Bailey, *Battles for Atlanta*: 95.

184. Bailey, *Battles for Atlanta*: 136.

185. Bailey, *Battles for Atlanta*: 140.

186. Nevin, *Sherman's March*: 51.

187. Nevin, *Sherman's March*: 54.

188. Gragg, *The Illustrated Confederate Reader*: 205.

189. Bailey, *Battles for Atlanta*: 26.

190. Bailey, *Battles for Atlanta*: 35.

191. Time Life Books, *Charleston—Voices*: 118.

192. Bailey, *Battles for Atlanta*: 39.

193. Botkin, *A Civil War Treasury*: 377-378.

194. Bailey, *Battles for Atlanta*: 71.

195. Time Life Books, *Atlanta—Voices*: 79.

196. McClellan, *I Rode with Jeb Stuart*: 417.

197. Time Life Books, *Atlanta—Voices*: 86.

198. Korn, *The Fight for Chattanooga*: 95.

199. Korn, *The Fight for Chattanooga*: 99.

200. Time Life Books, *Atlanta—Voices*: 76

201. Jaynes, *The Killing Ground*: 38.

202. Zwemer, *For Home and the Southland*: 54.

203. Time Life Books, *Wilderness—Voices*: 144.
204. Botkin, *A Civil War Treasury*: 483.
205. Time Life Books, *Wilderness—Voices*: 157.
206. Time Life Books, *Shenandoah 1862—Voices*: 77.
207. Thomas, *Robert E. Lee*: 332-333.
208. Botkin, *A Civil War Treasury*: 496.
209. Jaynes, *The Killing Ground*: 45.
210. Davis, *Death in the Trenches*: 115.
211. Davis, *Death in the Trenches*: 156.
212. Power, *Lee's Miserables*: 83.
213. Power, *Lee's Miserables*: 93-94.
214. Thomas, *Robert E. Lee*: 354.
215. Thomas, *Robert E. Lee*: 354.
216. Korn, *Pursuit to Appomattox*: 136.
217. Thomas, *Robert E. Lee*: 372.
218. Thomas, *Robert E. Lee*: 397.
219. Thomas, *Robert E. Lee*: 401.
220. Thomas, *Robert E. Lee*: 409.
221. Watkins, *CO. Aytch*: 21.
222. Korn, *The Fight for Chattanooga*: 25.
223. Nevin, *Sherman's March*: 36.
224. Gragg, *The Illustrated Confederate Reader*: 92-93.
225. Korn, *Pursuit to Appomattox*: 55.
226. Crocker, *Robert E. Lee on Leadership*: 226.
227. Korn, *Pursuit to Appomattox*: 117.
228. Korn, *Pursuit to Appomattox*: 16-17.
229. Gowan, *Stories, Anecdotes and Humor from the Civil War*: 20-21.
230. Thomas, *Robert E. Lee*: 352.
231. Davis, *First Blood*: 119.

# BIBLIOGRAPHY

Adelman, Gary E. "Hazletts Battery at Gettysburg." *Gettysburg Magazine* 21 (1999).

Bailey, Ronald H. *Battles for Atlanta*. Alexandria: Time Life Books, 1985.

———, *Bloodiest Day*. Alexandria: Time Life Books, 1984.

———, *Forward to Richmond*. Alexandria: Time Life Books, 1983.

Bedwell, Randall, ed. *May I Quote You General Lee?* Nashville: Cumberland House Publishing, 1997.

Botkin, B. A., ed. *A Civil War Treasury of Tales, Legends & Folklore*. New York: Random House, 1960.

Burns, Ken. *The Civil War: A Film by Ken Burns*. Ken Burns/Florentine Production, 1990.

Caroli, Betty B. *Inside The White House: First 200 Years*. New York: Canopy Books, 1992.

Channing, Steven A. *Confederate Ordeal*. Alexandria: Time Life Books, 1984.

Clark, Champ. *Gettysburg*. *Alexandria:* Time Life Books, 1984.

Crocker, H. W. *Robert E. Lee on Leadership*. Rocklin, Calif.: Prima Publishing, 1999.

Davis, William C. *Death in the Trenches*. Alexandria: Time Life Books, 1986.

———, *First Blood*. Alexandria: Time Life Books, 1983.

Freeman, Douglas S. *R. E. Lee*. New York: Charles Scribner's Sons, 1961.

Gragg, Rod. *The Illustrated Confederate Reader*. New York: Harper & Row, 1989.

Goolrich, William K. *Rebels Resurgent*. Alexandria: Time Life Books, 1985.

Gowan, Hugh. *Stories, Anecdotes and Humor from the Civil War*. Martinsburg, Penn.: Daisy Publications, 1983.

Hassler, William W. *Colonel John Pelham: Lee's Boy Artillerist*. Chapel Hill, N.C.: The University of North Carolina Press, 1960.

Jackson, Donald D. *Twenty Million Yankees*. Alexandria: Time Life Books, 1984.

Jaynes, Gregory, et. al. *The Killing Ground.* Alexandria: Time Life Books, 1984.

Johnson, Robert U. and Clarence C. Buel, eds. *Battles and Leaders of the Civil War.* New York: The Century Magazine, 1887.

Joslyn, Mauriel P., ed. *A Meteor Shining Brightly.* Milledgeville, Ga.: Terrell House Publishing, 1997.

Korn, Jerry. *The Fight for Chattanooga.* Alexandria: Time Life Books, 1985.

_____, *Pursuit to Appomattox.* Alexandria: Time Life Books, 1986.

McClellan, H. B. *I Rode with Jeb Stuart.* New York: DA Capo Press, 1994.

Nevin, David. *Sherman's March.* Alexandria: Time Life Books, 1986.

_____, *The Road to Shiloh.* Alexandria: Time Life Books, 1983.

Pfanz, Harry W. *Gettysburg—Culp's Hill & Cemetery Hill.* Chapel Hill, N.C.: The University of North Carolina Press, 1993.

Power, J. Tracy. *Lee's Miserables.* Chapel Hill, N.C.: The University of North Carolina Press, 1998.

Rhodes, Robert Hunt, ed. *All for the Union, The Civil War Diary and Letters of Elisha Hunt Rhodes.* New York: Orion Books, 1985.

Robertson, James I. Jr. *Stonewall Jackson.* New York: MacMillan Publishing USA, 1997.

_____, *Tenting Tonight.* Alexandria: Time Life Books, 1984.

Sears, Stephen W. *Landscape Turned Red—The Battle of Antietam.* Boston: Houghton Mifflin Company, 1983.

Shaara, Michael. *The Killer Angels.* New York: Ballentine Books, 1974.

Street, James J. *The Struggle for Tennessee.* Alexandria: Time Life Books, 1984.

Thomas, Emory M. *Robert E. Lee.* New York: W. W. Norton, 1995.

Time Life Books, eds. *Antietam—Voices of the Civil War.* Alexandria: Time Life Books, 1996.

_____, *Atlanta—Voices of the Civil War.* Alexandria: Time Life Books, 1996.

_____, *The Blockade.* Alexandria: Time Life Books, 1983

_____, *Chancellorsville—Voices of the Civil War.* Alexandria: Time Life Books, 1996.

_____, *Charleston—Voices of the Civil War*. Alexandria: Time Life Books, 1997.

_____, *Chattanooga—Voices of the Civil War*. Alexandria: Time Life Books, 1998.

_____, *Gettysburg—Voices of the Civil War*. Alexandria: Time Life Books, 1995.

_____, *Lee Takes Command*. Alexandria: Time Life Books, 1984.

_____, *Second Manassas—Voices of the Civil War*. Alexandria: Time Life Books, 1995.

_____, *Shenandoah 1862—Voices of the Civil War*. Alexandria: Time Life Books, 1997.

_____, *Shiloh—Voices of the Civil War*. Alexandria: Time Life Books, 1996.

_____, *Soldier Life—Voices of the Civil War*. Alexandria: Time Life Books, 1996.

_____, *Spies, Scouts and Raiders*. Alexandria: Time Life Books, 1985.

_____, *The Blockade*. Alexandria: Time Life Books, 1983.

_____, *Vicksburg—Voices of the Civil War*. Alexandria: Time Life Books, 1997.

_____, *Wilderness—Voices of the Civil War*. Alexandria: Time Life Books, 1998.

Trulock, Alice Rains. *In the Hands of Providence*. Chapel Hill, N.C.: The University of North Carolina Press, 1992.

Verdery, James Paul. *The Letters of James Paul Verdery*. Durham, N.C.: Special Collections Library at Duke University.

Watkins, Sam R. *CO. Aytch: A Confederate's Memoir of the Civil War*. Nashville: Cumberland Presbyterian Publishing House, 1882. Reprint, Dayton: Morningside Bookshop, 1982.

Zwemer, John. *For Home and the Southland*. Baltimore: Butternut and Blue Publishing Company, 1999.

**JOHN ZWEMER** is a contributor to *America's Civil War* magazine and has authored a regimental history titled *For Home and the Southland, A History of the 48th Georgia Infantry*. He is currently compiling a history of the USS *Augusta* and a Civil War diary of two Georgia brothers. John's deep appreciation of history extends to his thirty-year career as a history teacher in Georgia and the Carolinas. He is the originator of a dramatic presentation entitled *1865— A Soldier's Story* which enhances the experiences described in *A Civil War Pocket Reader*.

**PATRICK GORMAN** is a member of the Academy of Motion Picture Arts and Sciences and has been a professional actor for more than 50 years. He enthralled audiences with his portrayal of General John Bell Hood in the acclaimed movie *Gettysburg*.

To arrange for a dramatic presentation taken from *A Civil War Pocket Reader*, contact Stories of America, 535 River Cove Road, Social Circle, Georgia 30025.

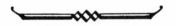